HONDURAS
& BELIZE

WHITE STAR
PUBLISHERS

HONDURAS & BELIZE

A

TEXTS AND PHOTOGRAPHS
Roberto Rinaldi

GRAPHIC DESIGN
Monica Morelli

FISH CHARTS
Angelo Mojetta

TRANSLATION
Studio Traduzioni Vecchia, Milan

B

C

D

© 2003 White Star S.r.l.
Via Candido Sassone, 22-24
13100 Vercelli, Italy
www.whitestar.it

ISBN 88-544-0057-2
REPRINTS:
1 2 3 4 5 6   09 08 07 06 05
Printed in China
Color separation: Grafotitoli Bassoli, Milan

1. Sponges in a
thousand different
species, crystalline
water, vertical walls:
in a nutshell, this
describes the extensive
coral reef that snakes
past the countries of
Honduras and Belize.

2–3. The seabeds off
Roatan Island are
some of the most
beautiful in the entire
Caribbean.

A. A Nassau grouper
on the reef off the
coast of Roatan.

B. This gorgonia
(Pterogorgia sp.) can
be seen at Turneffe
Island Atoll in Belize.

C. Gigantic sponges
and gorgonians grow
at Mary's Place, one
of Roatan's most
beautiful diving areas.

D. A vibrant yellow
Aplysina sponge stands
out on the sea floor in
the clear waters of
Glover's Reef.

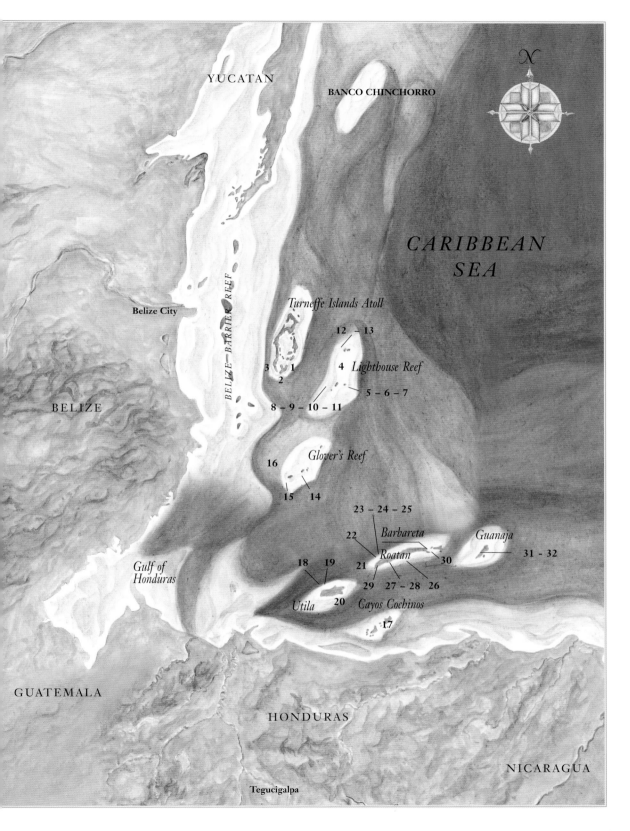

YUCATAN

BANCO CHINCHORRO

CARIBBEAN
SEA

Belize City

BELIZE—BARRIER REEF

Turneffe Islands Atoll

12 – 13

3 1   4 Lighthouse Reef
2

5 – 6 – 7

8 – 9 – 10 – 11

BELIZE

Glover's Reef

16

15   14

23 – 24 – 25

22   Barbareta   Guanaja
          Roatan
21   30   31 - 32

18   19
                               29   27 – 28   26

Gulf of
Honduras

Utila   20   Cayos Cochinos

17

GUATEMALA

HONDURAS

NICARAGUA

Tegucigalpa

5

INTRODUCTION

A

Honduras and Belize—two Central American countries on the Caribbean Sea—were for centuries linked by the same name, with Belize known as British Honduras until 1981. For divers, Honduras and Belize are still linked, by a large coral reef—the second largest in the world, after the Great Barrier Reef in Australia. The greater part of this coral structure borders the coast of Belize from north to south, creating coral atolls and at least 450 *cayes*, the local name for the tiny, sandy islands that emerge from the ocean above the coral. The reef then curves east, where it surrounds the magnificent Bay Islands of Honduras.

A. A mimetic toadfish waits motionless for prey to be attracted by a decoy, the antennae moving above its mouth.

B. The lagoon across from the small island of Half Moon Caye, in Belize.

B

C   D

C. The Bay Islands in Honduras are quite diverse, but are generally rocky and covered with luxuriant vegetation.

D. The magnificent beach on Lighthouse Reef Island, north of the atoll of the same name.

Though Honduras and Belize are quite distinct as countries—the first has a Spanish culture, the second English—they do share the same large, rich, unspoiled coral reef along their coasts, so we cover them both in the same dive guide. Though ordinary tourists could try to visit both of these countries in one vacation, we suggest that diving enthusiasts decide beforehand which country to visit first, and which to save for another trip. You'll want to spend a week in the water and a week in the interior of one of these fascinating countries to savor the allure of the immense tropical forests, the Mayan ruins rising above the treetops, and the colorful life in the realm of corals.

In both Belize and Honduras, you can find accommodations on the mainland and take daily sea excursions, or choose a week-long cruise on a live-aboard. Belize has three of the four coral atolls in the entire Caribbean Sea, while in Honduras all the most interesting diving areas are around the Bay Islands, already mentioned above. This is why, of the many dives possible in the two countries, in Belize we selected those directly accessible by live-aboards or

E

E. Belize has a rich heritage of ancient Mayan civilization. This is at Cahal Pech.

A

B

C

*A. Schools of yellow jacks (*Caranx bartholomaei*) are an extremely common sight both in the Bay Islands and along the reefs of Belize.*

B. In this photo of Roatan's seabed with its colorful sponges and gorgonians, a fire coral covers the skeleton of a dead gorgonian.

C. The walls of Lighthouse Reef have absolutely vertical areas that alternate with zones where coral promontories extend out to the open sea.

D. Dives along the reefs of Belize often feature crevices in the corals that drop right into the middle of the wall.

D

from accommodations in a resort on a caye within the atoll itself, while we suggest the Bay Islands of Honduras to those who want to go diving, but also want to savor the Caribbean way of life.

The climate is quite pleasant year-round in both countries. The outside temperature stays between 75 and 86 °F (24 to 30 °C), while a gentle breeze always makes your stay pleasant. Water temperature is between 79 and 84 °F (26 to 29 °C). Visibility depends more on general conditions at the time, but is usually excellent. It is, however, generally more rainy in the autumn, while June to November is the hurricane season.

All said, we hope that the following pages will give you a thorough picture of what to expect from the underwater world of these two countries, and wish you a pleasant vacation.

E. A tree trunk washed up by the sea on magnificent West End Bay beach in Roatan.

F. This enormous barrel sponge comes into sight during a dive along the seabeds off the southern coast of Roatan.

INTRODUCTION
Belize

A

The Republic of Belize, independent from the United Kingdom since 1981, is bordered by Mexico to the south, Honduras to the north, and Guatemala to the east. Its western coast faces the Caribbean Sea, with the entire coastline running north to south, and its famous coral reef, the second largest barrier reef in the world, snakes along parallel to it. Divers who want to explore the coral kingdom will find a wealth of accommodations to choose from. Many areas are now well-known tourist towns that thrive on the growing popularity of scuba diving, a driving economic force and significant source of income. Ambergris Caye, Placencia, and Belize City, site of the international airport, are points of departure for scuba divers.

Many diving areas along the lengthy coral reef, especially along the steep walls of the atolls that emerge from the deep sea off the reef, can be reached from the locations noted above. This is why we have decided to focus primarily on the three atolls of Glover's, Lighthouse Reef, and Turneffe Islands; they are accessible from either the mainland or the resorts on the sandy islands within the atolls that offer scuba diving cruise boats. We've intentionally left out diving areas within the reef closest to the coast so that we can devote more attention to those that are accessible from all departure points.

It's worthwhile to note, however, that many diving areas along the reef bordering Ambergris Caye are ideal for both snorkeling and scuba diving.

A. There is a wonderful resort on little Lighthouse Island, north of the atoll of the same name.

B. Another expressive image of the splendid sea off Lighthouse Reef and its coral islands, covered with palms and jungles.

C. We are moored off Half Moon Caye, on a seabed several feet deep, covered with pure white sand. This is the departure point for many magnificent dives.

D. This is the far northern tip of Lighthouse Reef. The photo was taken from the top of the key lighthouse that signals the reef to navigators.

E. From above an altar, a view of the archaeological site of Cahal Pech in the country's interior.

B

There are dense mangrove forests within the reef, especially along the coasts of the islands across from Belize City, which is home to friendly manatees that the Audubon Society is in the process of adopting. Though it is quite uncommon for divers to see manatees, it's a different story if you want to swim with whale sharks. The best place to find them is Placencia from April to May, when the largest fish in the world swim by here.

Aside from mammals and whale sharks, the sea off Belize owes its fame to the mysterious Blue Hole, an immense karstic cavity explored in 1970 by Jacques Cousteau's team. It opens right in the middle of the outermost reef off Lighthouse Reef Atoll, and offers magnificent sights.

Like Turneffe Islands and Glover's Reef atolls, the seabeds of Lighthouse plunge abruptly down, creating impressive walls rich with benthic life and fish. As we have noted, Lighthouse is accessible from Ambergris Caye, Belize City, and resorts on Lighthouse and Turneffe cayes. You can't leave Belize without diving Blue Hole at least once. Lighthouse and Turneffe are very close to each other and are accessible from land, resorts on the atolls, or live-aboards. Glover's Atoll is farther south and less accessible, due to its distance from Ambergris Caye and Belize City. It is also off the routes of live-aboards. Stay in a resort on the sands of one of the cayes within it and pay it a special visit.

A. This dive is named after the old turtle that lives in this area, shown here with the diver.

B. A gigantic Ectyoplasia sponge has colonized the coral wall.

Myrtle's Turtle
Turneffe Islands Atoll

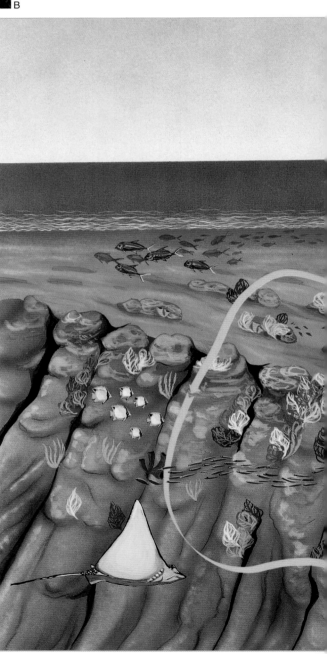

You are in the immediate vicinity of the southern tip of Turneffe Atoll, facing the eastern side. The diving point is easy to find, thanks to two metallic structures from the old lighthouse on the lower part of the reef. The mooring point is located near the area where the slope that connects the plateau, with an average depth of 35 to 55 feet (11 to 18 meters), breaks off from the detrital bank, which begins at around 60 to 75 feet (20 to 25 meters).

As soon as you enter the water, you'll note the teeming life of the plateau, and will be struck by the sight of a veritable forest of gorgonians that make up for their drab light brown and green coloring with their wild variety of forms. Finish your exploration of this part of the seabed when the depth begins to increase and head straight for the drop-off. This is obviously where the sea floor is at its richest, but the steep slope and clear water, brightly illuminated even at significant depths, make it easy to inadvertently go too deep for a recreational dive, so be careful.

Here imposing coral promontories interrupt the regularity of the edge and extend out into the open sea. Most coral life concentrates around these

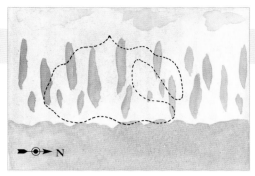

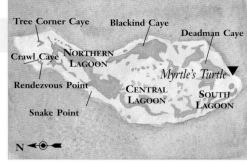

Tree Corner Caye   Blackind Caye

Deadman Caye

Crawl Caye   **NORTHERN LAGOON**

Myrtle's Turtle ▼

Rendezvous Point   **CENTRAL LAGOON**

SOUTH LAGOON

Snake Point

N

36 ft
11 m

59 ft
18 m

80 ft
25

B

structures. You'll find a number of barrel and organ-pipe sponges, an enormous mass of bright red sponges, great gorgonian fans, and beautiful tufts of black coral. Soldierfish and yellow snappers add to the beauty of the area, which is also an ideal place to see eagle rays. Another typical inhabitant of these waters is Myrtle the turtle, a large turtle who has been spotted here regularly for about fifteen years. Myrtle is sometimes very friendly, but can also be a bit shy. You may see her along the outer wall or on the reef plateau, or even in the

A

D

E

F

G

area closer to exposed land, where there is an algae meadow.

As you ascend, always try to reserve some time for the rich plateau. Carefully explore among the gorgonians and sponges, because this is a perfect place to find and photograph many small creatures. You'll discover a profusion of flamingo tongues, as well as many small shrimp and other crustaceans. This is also an ideal place to look for the whitespotted toadfish, which is endemic to Belize. You'll find it hidden motionless under the rocks or in cracks, displaying its large mouth adorned with a profusion of barbels.

C

A. A rocky spur with a wealth of sponges and gorgonians at a depth of about 100 feet (30 meters).

B. A barrel sponge in a deeper part of the reef.

C. A large turtle, startled out of a crevice in the coral reef, slowly moves away.

D. Sometimes the creatures of the coral reef engage in silent but brutal battles for space: here, the branches of a gorgonian traverse the body of a sponge.

E. The splendid toadfish (Sanopus splendidus) and a typical creature of these waters, lies motionless under a rock.

F. A characteristic nocturnal encounter: the arrow crab, Stenorhynchus seticornis.

G. Gorgonia flabellum is a typical inhabitant of the shallower areas of Caribbean reefs.

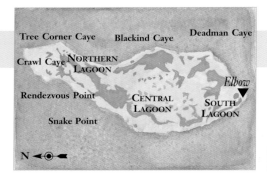

Tree Corner Caye
Blackind Caye
Deadman Caye
Crawl Caye
NORTHERN LAGOON
Rendezvous Point
CENTRAL LAGOON
Snake Point
Elbow
SOUTH LAGOON
N

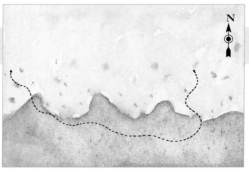

N

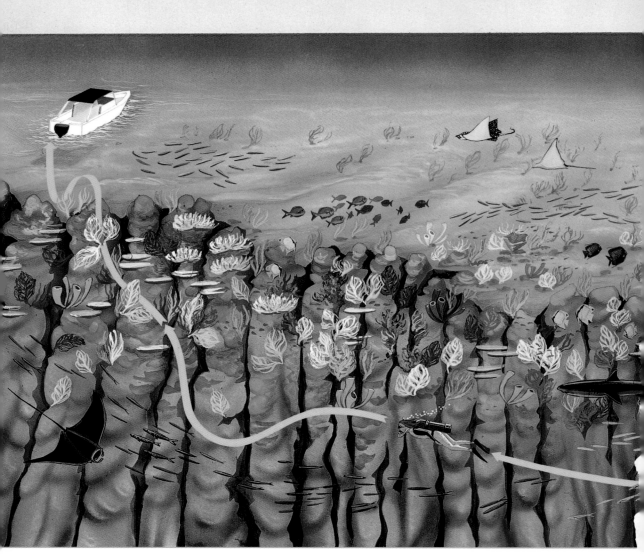

A. The distinctive abundance of pelagic fish like these jacks is what makes dives at Elbow so famous and popular.

B. Swept by powerful currents, some areas of this underwater wall at Turneffe Reef are quite spectacular.

A

B

Elbow
Turneffe Islands Atoll

A dive at Elbow is quite distinctive for the sea around Belize. Although it is one of the most beautiful dives anywhere in Belize, many operators prefer to avoid it because of the difficult conditions they often encounter. The dive takes place along the reef that surrounds Turneffe Island, right at its southern tip.

Elbow is actually quite descriptive of the area where the dive begins. Here, the reef drastically changes course to create an underwater promontory, a place where powerful currents sweep past, making this a classic drift dive, where the diver jumps into the water from the boat and allows himself to be carried by the current. When the dive is over, the boat will pick you up a few hundred meters away. This is one of the reasons why many dive operators, especially those with large cruise boats, prefer to avoid this site. It would be extremely difficult for a large yacht to pick up scattered scuba divers who surface in different areas of the ocean. The flow of the current, which usually runs from the north, and the fact that this point is highly exposed often create surf in this area.

Another factor that makes this a dive for experts is the rather significant

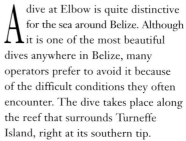

60 ft
18 m

100 ft
30 m

A

depth that needs to be maintained, since the shallowest part of the reef is between 60 and 100 feet (18 to 30 meters) deep. Of course, if the descent goes to a depth of 130 feet (39 meters), the top of the reef at 100 feet (30 meters) will stop you from making a multilevel dive, and you'll have to make decompression stops. These stops must be conducted in the open sea in the current. This justifies the hesitancy of certain operators to take you to Elbow.

That said, let's see what awaits you underwater. As noted, everyone must be ready together, properly equipped, and prepared to plunge right to the top of the reef immediately after jumping in, to prevent the current

from carrying you far from the top of the wall and forcing you to abandon the dive. So descend quickly, until you reach the top of the wall between 65 and 100 feet (20 and 30 meters) down.

You'll immediately realize that something strange is going on in these waters. You can tell by the odd move-ments of the fish—from tiny reef fish to predators like snappers or jacks— and the frenetic activity that animates the top reef. You'll immediately understand why the current is truly the breath of life, sweeping through the coral reef and completely trans-forming it. Elbow has gorgonians that some say are larger than anywhere else in the Caribbean, with fans that extend into the current.

B

C

Once you're in the middle of the wall, you can easily duck out of the current, as the wall is extremely complex and offers a thousand crevices where you can find protection and calm water—but remember that the current is usually moving from north to south, and thus sweeps past both sides. In addition to gorgonians, a dive at Elbow means that breathtaking encounters are possible, and you may be lucky enough to experience the thrill of an extraordinary sight. If you talk to local divers, you're sure to meet someone who has swum with fifty eagle rays, or encountered gigantic mantas or sharks seen nowhere else.

E

D

F

A. A magnificent organ-pipe sponge rises from the floor, while the current ruffles the gorgonian branches on the seabed.

B. It's quite common to see eagle rays when diving on the reefs of Belize; at Elbow, their presence is practically guaranteed.

C. Two large French angelfish (Pomacanthus paru) *swim in the shallower part of the reef.*

D. A grouper hidden in a crevice uses the services of a cleaner fish.

E. A dense school of Bermuda chub (Kyphosus sectatrix) *rises from the coral floor to the surface.*

F. Another image of the wall with its abundant display of sponges and gorgonians, photographed here at a depth of over 100 feet (30 meters).

G. A trumpetfish (Aulostomus maculatus) *attempts to hide among the branches of a gorgonian, but the camera flash reveals its reddish color.*

G

Tree Corner Caye   Blackind Caye

Deadman Caye

Crawl Caye

NORTHERN LAGOON

Rendezvous Point

CENTRAL LAGOON

SOUTH LAGOON

Snake Point

Sayonara

N

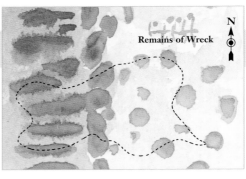

Remains of Wreck

N

A. A magnificent, gigantic Aplysina sponge rises from the sloping floor at Sayonara.

B. Sea plumes are also quite common along the slope, which descends gently and steadily from a depth of 65 feet (20 meters).

A

B

66 ft
20 m

116 ft
35 m

Sayonara
Turneffe Atoll

This is in the southern part of Turneffe Reef, on the western side. The dive at Sayonara is not the most beautiful that Belize has to offer, but it is still worth mentioning because it is often the first dive offered at the beginning of a live-aboard trip. The name of this diving area comes from the wreck of an old cargo boat, the *Sayonara*, which was sunk here in 1985. The wreck, of no interest to scuba divers, is now reduced to a shapeless mass of rubble.

The fixed mooring line for the *Wave Dancer*, one of the most famous live-aboards in the area, is very near the wreck. The mooring point is about 50 feet (15 meters) deep, the average depth of the extensive, flat reef. Jump in from the boat right here. The environment is immediately quite rich; you can't help but notice a large number of pale violet Caribbean sea feathers (*Pseudopterogorgia* sp.), as well as barrel sponges, pink cylinder-shaped sponges, and red arborescent sponges. Fish life is also quite rich and varied. You'll have no problem spotting emperor angelfish and queen angelfish, as well as a profusion of butterflyfish, especially the banded and spotfin butterflies, which almost always swim in pairs. During our first

A

B

C

D

E

A. This gigantic spherical sponge is right on the plateau several feet from the fixed mooring point.

B. This yellow elephant ear sponge (Agelas sp.) stands out on the seabed at Sayonara.

C. Spectacular tube sponges (Callyspongia) kindle to a lovely pink in the camera flash.

D. This is a good example of the seabeds at Sayonara, with barren detrital-sedimentary areas alternating with regions full of animal life.

E. This seahorse has made its permanent home near the plateau's mooring point, several feet deep.

dive at Sayonara, a small group of amberjacks immediately swam after us. On the sand, you can see numerous yellowhead jawfish and small blennies who have adapted to life under the sand.

But don't be distracted by what's happening on the plateau. Swim west, following the gentle slope. Very soon you'll be facing a clear drop-off beyond which the slope of the sea floor grows considerably steeper, between 65 and 82 feet (20 to 25 meters) deep. Go deeper to 115 feet (35 meters) to enjoy everything this seabed has to offer. The slope is mostly detrital and sandy, but still full of areas with sponges, gorgonians, and corals. Often just several feet beyond the drop-off, visibility changes drastically, and you may find yourself immersed in magnificent blue, completely crystalline water.

If you reached your depth quickly, you can swim around at this depth to fully enjoy the beauty of this part of the seabed. Otherwise, it is best to stop for a few minutes at your maximum depth and then complete your dive as you ascend. Although the sponges and gorgonians are large and will certainly attract your attention, don't forget to carefully observe the tiny life forms.

You'll find a profusion of violet-and-yellow fairy basslets, triggerfish, smooth trunkfish, and pufferfish. The white-and-beige gorgonian branches offer an ideal environment for mimetic trumpetfish.

While at your depth, swimming in the limpid water, always pay attention to what's happening overhead—it's not at all uncommon to see spectacular eagle rays in this part of the sea. Ascend along the slope and come back to the surface of the plateau. Spend some time between the mooring platform and the remains of the wreck, where you can often find a seahorse.

F

G

F. There is no longer
anything of interest in
the wreck of the old
ship that gives this
diving area its name.

G. A sponge and deep-
water sea fan rise
from a section of the
coral floor separated
from the detrital slope.

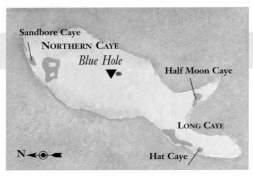

Sandbore Caye
NORTHERN CAYE
Blue Hole
Half Moon Caye
LONG CAYE
Hat Caye
N

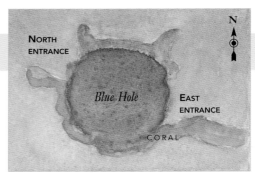

NORTH ENTRANCE
Blue Hole
EAST ENTRANCE
CORAL
N

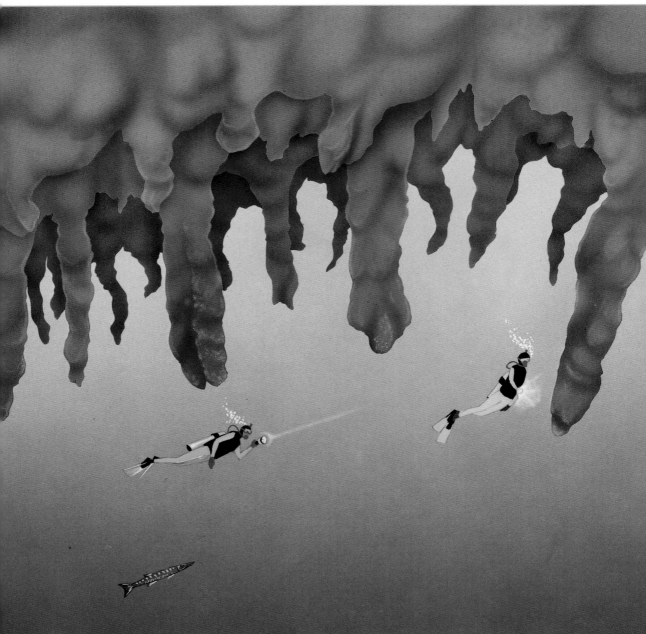

A. The dive at Blue Hole is indisputably Belize's most famous. Enormous stalactites hang from the rocky vault about 130 feet (39 meters) deep.

B. The magnificence of this place is what makes a dive at Blue Hole so beautiful.

A

B

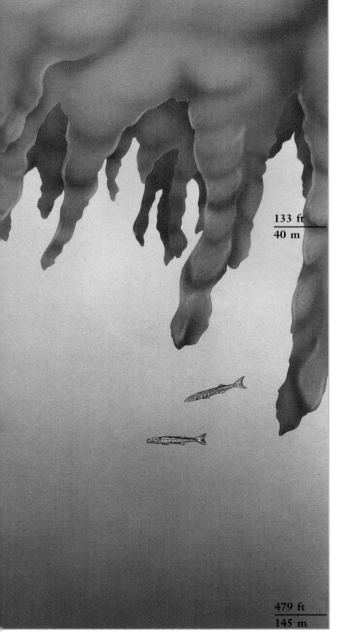

133 ft
40 m

479 ft
145 m

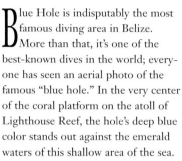

Blue Hole
Lighthouse Reef

Blue Hole is indisputably the most famous diving area in Belize. More than that, it's one of the best-known dives in the world; everyone has seen an aerial photo of the famous "blue hole." In the very center of the coral platform on the atoll of Lighthouse Reef, the hole's deep blue color stands out against the emerald waters of this shallow area of the sea.

This geological phenomenon, at first inexplicable, was made famous by Jacques Cousteau back in 1970. The funnel-shaped hole gaping in the reef, about a quarter mile in diameter, plunges down for well over 350 feet (110 meters), with its diameter enlarging as it descends. It was difficult for the *Calypso* to navigate the shallow coral waters and enter the basin above the hole, and today visitors still follow the same route on both the day boats from the coast or resorts on the islands of the atolls and on the larger liveaboards. The southern edge is used for small boats, while the opposite side is for the big charter yachts.

Once you reach the place, you'll immediately note that the edges of the Blue Hole do not plunge immediately into the abyss, but briefly connect with the coral plateau. This shallow, flat sea floor is where guides instruct

A

B

A. An inexperienced diver could be disconcerted by the majestic atmosphere, the darkness, and the depth of the sea here. Follow the guide's instructions to the letter.

B. Calcareous formations hang from the ceiling of this impressive overturned funnel. You need to know the place well to find the most spectacular point.

divers to make their final equipment checks and relax before they descend into the abyss. As you swim toward the edge, you'll notice that you're moving toward a hole that looks more black than blue, swallowing the sunlight without a trace. The impression of pitch-black darkness creates a powerful feeling that you can't shake, since the light vanishes into the abyss without bouncing back to your eyes. Yet you sense light and clear water as soon as an object, your companion, or the rocky wall, appears before your eyes. The walls plummet vertically, creating an impressive cliff, and you

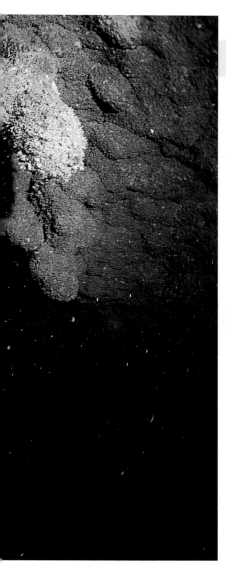

C. Fish feeding was once practiced on the side where smaller boats moor, which explains why this is the only place where fish and a few small sharks still show up today.

D. Due to the depth, dives at Blue Hole are just a few minutes long, but it's worth the effort.

D

feel as if you're descending into the center of the earth. This is what awaits you in a dive into Blue Hole: a whirl of powerful, unexpected sensations that completely overwhelm you; you'll have to abandon yourself here if you want to enjoy this dive.

At about 130 feet (39 meters) deep, the precipice forms a sandy ledge that hangs suspended over the abyss, from which spectacular stalactites hang. These stalactites tell the story of Blue Hole and its origins. Imagine an ancient coral reef that developed and prospered, producing a large mass of carbonate rock. Then imagine the

arrival of a glacial period that caused the water to recede hundreds of feet from the shoreline, leaving the ancient reef exposed like a mountain of limestone. Then the rains came, carving into the limestone and dissolving the calcium carbonate, just like a karstic cave, and forming the hole. Afterward, waters supersaturated with calcium carbonate deposited the mineral, creating spectacular stalactites, which can form only in a subaerial environment, not underwater. Then another change in the shoreline covered everything with ocean water, creating what we see today. As we have said, the marvelous stalactites are at a depth of 103 feet (39 meters), and your dive should stop here. Usually, guides will not allow divers to spend more than ten minutes down here, and dives are always led in groups.

A

B

A. Beyond the flat, white sand area, a group of coral rocks rises from the floor before the wall drops off into the sea.

B. The sandy area increases in average depth before it reaches the coral rocks on the sea floor. There are many kinds of fish here, such as these snappers.

Eagle Landing
Lighthouse Reef

Here you are, moored on the southern side of Lighthouse Reef, where the corals form a large loop. If this were dry land, it would doubtless create a magnificent bay. But these are corals, and you'll waken from your reverie as the live-aboard *Wave Dancer* moors at the buoy. It seems suspended on the crystalline water, with the white sand floor and a pair of stingrays clearly visible below.

Jump into the water and swim to the shelf, identified by the dark blue color of the sea. Head due south. The sand on the seabed is at a depth of about 23 feet (7 meters). You can easily see many of the burrows made by stingrays, and large Caribbean conches are abundant here. Glide out toward the open sea until you reach a coral ridge that runs approximately east-west. On the inner side of the coral—quite fragmented, complex, and covered by a myriad of gorgonians—the sand slopes to a depth of 30 feet (9 meters). Reef fish are abundant; colorful schools of chromis, little groups of yellow snappers, parrotfish, triggerfish, and many others make this part of the reef even more lively. This is an ideal place for anyone who wants to enjoy a shallow dive that still offers magnificent sights.

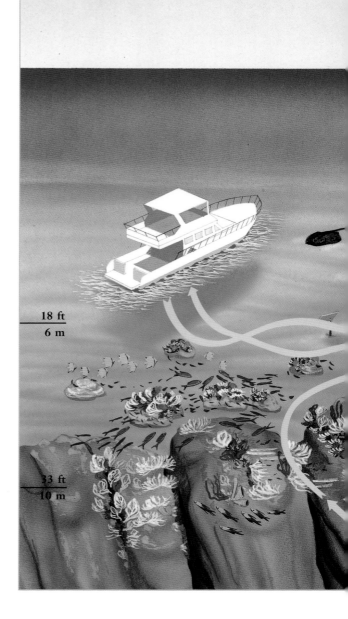

18 ft
6 m

33 ft
10 m

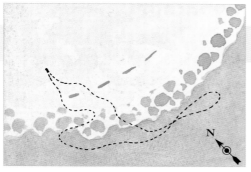

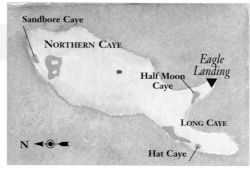

Sandbore Caye

NORTHERN CAYE

Half Moon
Caye

Eagle
Landing

LONG CAYE

Hat Caye

N

A

E

D. Elegant barracudas seem to enjoy the shade of the boat.

E. The coral ridge that rises from the sandy floor is often traversed by deep cracks running right to the middle of the wall.

F. Small, colorful Creole wrasses (Clepticus parrai) are everywhere, in little isolated groups among the rocks or in large schools near the walls and coral rocks.

G. Located in the area where the sand meets the coral ridge, a group of signs explains the biology of various marine creatures.

B

C

D

F

A. A lovely example of pillar coral right on the top of the ridge.

B. This is the beautiful wall that plunges vertically to the depths.

At times, it truly teems with incredible life.

C. Large tarpon habitually accompany divers as they explore Lighthouse Reef.

To the east of the great anchoring mass, you'll see something certain to draw your attention: a sign mounted as if on a music stand out on the white sand, facing the coral ridge. This is a series of signs, each describing a specific group—hard corals, gorgoni-

ans, sponges—and placed by a living example.

But let's return to the diving itinerary. When you get to the ridge, decide whether to stop and wander around at a shallow depth or descend to explore the great wall. The distinc-

tive feature of the place is the large abundance of stony corals that flourish here: the ridge is nothing more than a very jagged, chaotic mass of colonial coral structures. These reef-building corals grow by building their own limestone structure, which both adds to and changes those already on the seabed. This is why the crest is a continuous succession of peaks and fractures, which you can pass through, leading to the center of the wall in quite a spectacular fashion. The wall is extremely impressive and vertical. It is broken by coral promontories that correspond to the buttresses of the

upper ridge, with hollow areas similar to vertical valleys that generally correspond to the gaps in the coral. In the clear water of this sea, the wall plunges below you into total blackness. The grooves in the coral lead you to a depth of about 65 feet (20 meters)—

and you may even have descended a little farther—so it will be easy to spot portions of certain zones where the wall transforms into a steep slope before plunging vertically toward unsafe depths.

If you gaze down from above, you'll see that a deep dive is unnecessary here, with a sea floor that is at its most between 30 and 80 feet (9 to 24 meters). If you're observant, you'll note that even this outer slope has a large number of corals and stony formations, which are as common and abundant here as in any other place in the area.

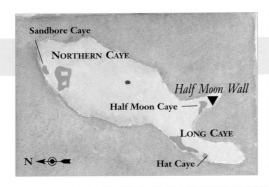

Sandbore Caye

NORTHERN CAYE

Half Moon Wall

Half Moon Caye —

LONG CAYE

Hat Caye

N

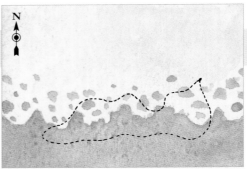

N

17 ft
5 m

35 ft
10 m

A. Numerous schools of jacks can be found near the wall at the far southeastern tip of Lighthouse Reef.

B. Impressive cracks in the coral rocks lead right to the center of one of the most beautiful walls in the Caribbean.

A

B

Half Moon Wall
Lighthouse Reef

Half Moon Wall is one of the most famous dives you can experience on the seabeds of Lighthouse Reef, or anywhere in Belize, for that matter. Once again, you'll find yourself anchored in that characteristic area where the reef near the lovely islet of Half Moon Caye curves before reaching its last southern offshoot, forming a distinct recess, almost a gulf facing south, after running for miles in a straight line from north to south. It's a fabulous place to moor your boat and relax for a few hours, as the extensive, shallow seabed of pure white sand gives the water an incredible emerald color that stands out vividly against the deep blue of the open sea.

Jump into the water with your boat moored. You'll immediately find yourself on a sandy, flat, broad seabed about 15 feet (5 meters) deep. On the sand, you'll see many imprints of stingrays and a multitude of conches, whose movements can be traced by the trail left on the sandy floor. Swim to the south, and you'll immediately discover a profusion of garden eels several feet from you. These long, thin sand eels protrude from the sand with most of their bodies, sinuously moving together. From a distance, they look like an expanse of sea grass

undulating with the tide. But as you gradually approach, the eels closest to you vanish rapidly under the sand, while the more distant ones continue to poke out, giving you the impression that you're swimming in place.

Still, as you gradually move south, the depth increases, and you'll exceed 30 feet (9 meters) on the sand before the floor once again rises before you. You'll find yourself before a reef of coral rock colonized by a multitude of sponges and gorgonians, growing up to about 16 feet (5 meters) from the surface. Beyond the reef, the famous, imposing wall awaits you. Climb up the coral buttresses, or enter one of the many narrow crevices that open in the reef, to experience the world of

this immense wall. It is luxuriant, vertical, and impressive, but owes much of its beauty and irresistible fascination to its position, which allows it to bask in light. So let yourself go, but keep an eye on your depth gauge, because the bright, transparent water could deceive you and draw you to unexpected depths.

There is a wealth of large black coral trees, every type of sponge, a profusion of gorgonians, but there are also large coral formations here. Hard corals colonize hundreds of square feet of wall, and in their turn are colonized by hydrozoans, tunicates, sponges, and more. At Half Moon Wall, it's worth the effort to go a little deeper than usual, to reach the realm of the great seabed groupers, which become truly gigantic here. This part of the sea is especially abundant in pelagic fish—and some feel it is the richest area anywhere near Lighthouse Reef. In addition to the usual schools of jacks, you may be lucky enough to spot eagle rays, mantas, or bull sharks.

Of course, the flip side to a deep dive is that your time in the water is drastically reduced. So remember to start your ascent in time, so you can enjoy the wall as you gradually decrease your depth. You'll finally reach the ridge at a depth of 20 feet (6 meters), where the spectacle of the colorful coral sea teeming with life awaits you with all its fascination and profusion of light and color.

A. Rather large reef-building corals are especially common in the shallower areas of the wall.

B. This is almost the summit of the ridge that seems to divide the coral lagoon from the vertical wall. The wealth of life forms competing for space is truly impressive.

C. Timid garden eels abound in sandy areas within the lagoon.

D. A school of tropical mullets swims among the corals several feet deep.

E. A tiny moray peeps from its den right in the middle of the wall.

F. Branching tube sponges (Pseudoceratina sp.) hang from the rocky vault that drops over Half Moon Wall.

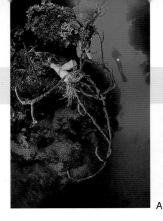

A. Red sponges from
the genus Aplysina
take advantage of the
current running
through a wide crack
in the corals.

B. In the middle of
the wall, several coral
promontories full of
sponges and stony
corals reach out to
the open sea.

Tarpon Cave
Lighthouse Reef

You're moored in the water off Lighthouse Reef, slightly west of the little sandy islet of Half Moon Caye. In a cruise boat, you can quickly take advantage of the good weather to head to Half Moon Caye and stop in the splendid lagoon for a couple of dives, which are definitely some of the best in the area.

Right below the boat, at a shallow depth, you'll find a vast meadow of ribbon-shaped algae flourishing on a flat seabed, with alternating wide patches of white sand. It seems of little interest to scuba divers, but will reward you with very interesting discoveries when you return to this depth after exploring the deeper parts of the wall. If the wind is pushing the boat to the opposite side of the reef, be careful not to lose your sense of direction as you swim over the flat floor with its algae and sand, in search of the coral wall. Orient yourself well before you jump into the water, and be sure you know what direction to take. If you have a compass, follow a 180° route south. In any case, if the southern wind pushes the stern of the boat toward land, probably the best thing to do is swim on the surface to the bow and descend along the moor- ing line, so you don't waste time and

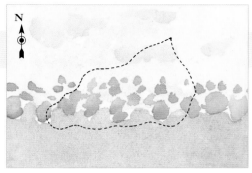

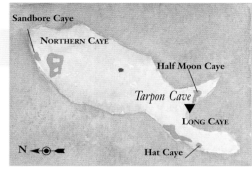

Sandbore Caye

NORTHERN CAYE

Half Moon Caye

Tarpon Cave

LONG CAYE

N

Hat Caye

17 ft
5 m

33 ft
10 m

A

B

C

precious air by swimming along the plateau, which you'll have plenty of time to visit on your return.

Descend quickly, heading toward the south, and note that after several feet, the algae make way for a steeper slope of white sand, with a depth between 23 and 50 feet (7 to 15 meters). You'll find yourself facing a spectacular coral ridge that runs east to west, rising several feet from the sandy floor and then plunging decisively toward the blue depths on the southern side. Near the coral rise, the sand accentuates the slope as you reach depths of 40 to 60 feet (12 to 18 meters).

On the sand, there are many beautiful coral masses covered with lovely sea feathers (*Pseudopterogorgia* sp.) or

sea fans (*Gorgonia* sp.). You may see a great number of reef fish here, such as gorgeous silver snappers that hover motionless under gorgonians or enjoy the services of cleaner fish and shrimp who efficiently remove their parasites. A fundamental characteristic of this dive, however, is the morphology of the coral ridge. As soon as you arrive, you'll note that it is carved with deep

A. Corals, gorgonians, and various types of sponges take advantage of the flat area that juts from the vertical wall.

B. A stingray seems to wait for scuba divers right under the boat moored on the sandy, shallow floor.

C. The ridge that separates the wall from the lagoon is covered with gorgonians: their elastic, flexible skeletons help them withstand the force of the current.

D. Multicolored sponges from the genus Aplysina *have colonized the wall.*

E. A detail of a brittle star grasping a red sponge.

*F. This sailfin blenny (*Emblemaria pandionis*) was very uncooperative about being photographed: it absolutely refused to open its spectacular dorsal fin.*

G. A red sponge grows on a barrel sponge.

canyons that look out to the deep blue sea. It is truly spectacular to swim through these canyons, their walls covered with sponges and gorgonians, and look out over the impressive wall that drops off into unfathomable depths.

Descend even deeper, leaving the crack in the coral behind you, and descend along the wall. The water will become even more pleasantly cool and clear, and beyond 100 feet (30 meters) it turns a magnificent, deep blue color. As always, it's not worth the trouble to push to great depths, as beyond a certain depth the seabed becomes bare and covered with a whitish sediment.

Stop at around 100 feet (30 meters) for a few minutes to admire the gigan-tic sponges and beautiful solitary gorgonian branches, and then slowly begin to move back up again. You'll soon reach the canyon area. Cross the canyons to return to the boat. Notice how the spectacle changes now that white sand rather than blue sea is before you at the exit from the crack. Stop near the coral ridge, with its wealth of fish, sponges, and gorgonians, but don't forget to leave a little air in your tanks so that you can explore the sand and grass beds before returning to the boat. With a little attention, you can discover entire stretches of seabed populated by colonies of garden eels, who emerge from the sea floor and seem to dance with the current. Lie on the seabed and be still: you'll quickly see them appear one after another, only to vanish as you exhale.

The sandy plateau is also populated by an enormous number of stingrays, some of which are gigantic. These are isolated individuals, often accompanied by a small jack hoping to snap up a few crumbs of food the stingray leaves behind. They are somewhat wary of divers, but with a bit of patience, you can try to get close enough to take a picture. Among the imprints that stingrays make in the sand, you'll be sure to notice the profusion of conches, whose shells are a symbol of the Caribbean Sea.

It's now time to get back to the boat. Don't be surprised if you see a large barracuda, hovering motionless in the shade of the keel, or a curious turtle swimming over from the surface.

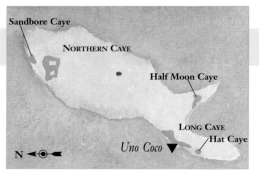

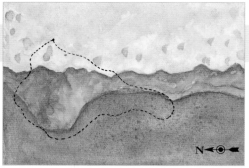

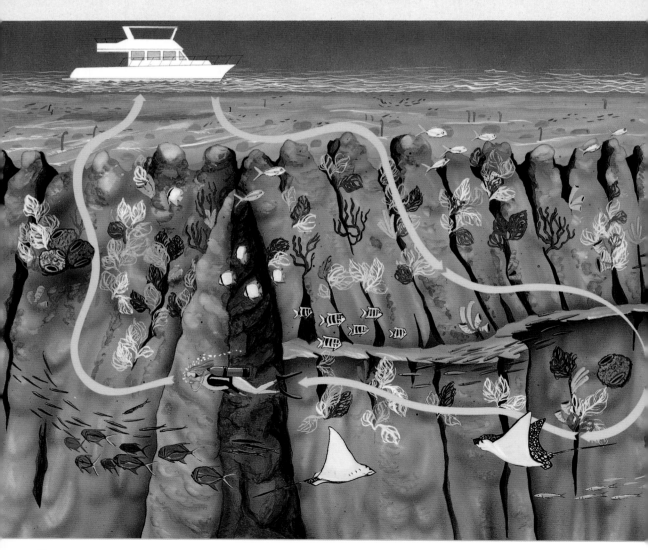

A. Here is one of the most beautiful sections of the entire dive. You'll find it by descending along the wall and heading south.

B. The area where the coral platform connects to the wall is extremely rich and interesting.

A

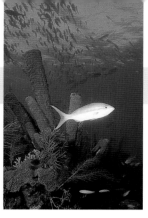

B

Uno Coco
Lighthouse Reef

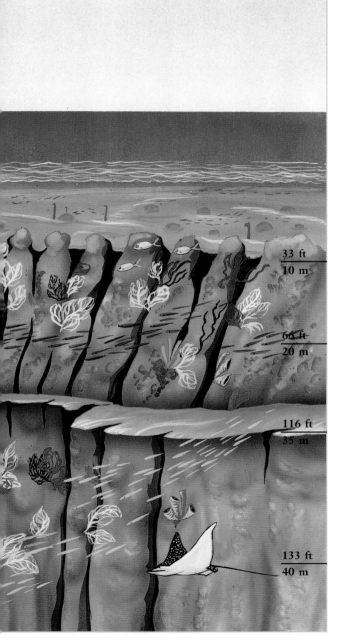

33 ft
10 m

66 ft
20 m

116 ft
35 m

133 ft
40 m

You're on the western side of Lighthouse Reef, at the southern tip of Long Caye. This area used to be known as Tres Cocos, because of the three palms that could clearly be seen on the beach. Then hurricane Mitch carried off two of them, leaving just one scraggly palm.

This is certainly one of the most beautiful dives near the atoll at Lighthouse—or at least one of the most colorful. You'll find large clusters of sponges in every shape and color, growing one atop another, rising from the floor, and hanging from the vaults of overhangs. Fish are abundant at Uno Coco as well, which you'll notice as soon as you jump into the water— you'll immediately be surrounded by a myriad of reef fish, including sergeant majors, yellowtail snappers, Bermuda chub, and yellow jacks. The flat seabed below, covered with masses of gorgonians, is broken into a series of stony coral peaks and valleys with white sand floors. Very often you'll see solitary barracudas, motionless in the shadow of gorgonians, who will allow you to approach without too much fuss. Photographers should try to take photographs right away, before the barracudas become irritated by divers arriving from the boat and swim away.

Proceed toward the edge of the reef. Here you can decide whether to head north or south. Usually, and with good reason, guides decide to begin the dive against the current and then float back down with it. Nevertheless, we feel that you should swim south to see the most beautiful part of the wall. Don't miss a special little corner of the seabed located due south of the wall, right where you arrive when you swim down from the boat. The area has been colonized by three or four enormous branches of colorful gorgonians and sponges, which range from light brown to lilac, yellow, and red. It's easy to find the place: just go to the edge and descend, keeping the wall to your left. The depth is between 40 and 60 feet (12 to 18 meters), and you'll know you're on the right

track when you see three large barrel sponges attached to each other, standing right before the group of gorgonians. Continue in that direction to find a profusion of colorful sponges and various gorgonians, as well as both pelagic and reef fish.

This is a good place to dive early in the day, when the bright, warm light from behind the wall makes it truly magical. In the early morning, you'll discover amberjacks hunting little sardines, anchovies, and mackerel, who flee in tight schools, all the fish standing out against the deep blue sea. This is also a likely spot to see the

eagle rays so typical of Lighthouse Reef, although they are unfortunately very timid and suspicious.

Continue to swim south, keeping the wall on your left. This is not really a wall, but a very steep slope that drops to a sandy plateau at a depth of over 130 feet (39 meters). If you continue, you'll come to a place where the slope seems to have been sliced with a knife, as if a giant had carried off a plug of

A. Colorful Creole wrasses are sometimes extremely abundant on this wall. This area is right before the coral plateau, ascending from the deep wall.

B. A dense school of yellow jacks almost always gathers below the boat, their numbers increasing with the strength of the current.

C

D

E

it. From a depth of about 115 feet (35 meters), the wall plunges steeply, creating a pronounced cavern that is quite impressive. This lovely sight is the only reason to descend farther, and in any event you should go no deeper than 130 feet (40 meters). Other than

that, the maximum recommended depth is 100 feet (30 meters). When you reach the large cavern, it's time to turn around and retrace your steps. You can ascend either diagonally along the wall, or directly over the coral plateau back to the boat.

C. Sponges seem to grow larger as the depth increases.

D. An example of the richness and color of the wall at Uno Coco, at a depth of about 80 feet (25 meters).

E. Solitary barracudas are a common sight on the coral plateau, especially at dusk.

F. The first dive of the day, when the warm light of dawn penetrates the surface of the sea, is an excellent time to find an abundance of fish.

G. Various types of sponges have taken residence in the skeleton of a gorgonian, away from the wall.

F

G

Sandbore Caye
NORTHERN CAYE
Half Moon Caye
LONG CAYE
Que Brada ▼
Hat Caye
N ←⊙→

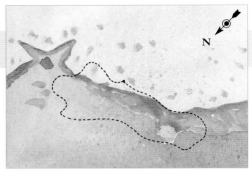

N

A. A large nocturnal crab wanders the sand on the sea floor.

B. After following the first part of the wall, find the point where it changes direction, which is populated by an abundance of benthic life.

A

B

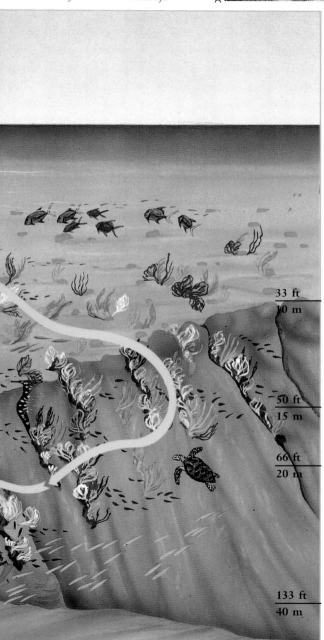

33 ft
10 m

50 ft
15 m

66 ft
20 m

133 ft
40 m

Que Brada
Lighthouse Reef

The boat is moored at the reef; with a little luck, you'll find the stern right at the coral's edge, where the plateau is transformed into a vertical wall, at times plunging steeply. To avoid straying from the dive plan described here, remember to head west to a stretch of wall that runs north to south. Descend along the wall to a depth of about 100 feet (30 meters). Below, you can clearly see the sandy floor between 165 and 200 feet (50 to 60 meters) down.

Beyond a depth of 130 feet (39 meters), the wall becomes rather bare except for a few large, solitary barrel sponges on the floor. But between 50 and 100 feet (15 to 30 meters), the wall is full of black coral, with a profusion of reddish or greenish branches that completely cover the rock. At the base of this forest of black and thorny corals grow many colorful sponges. Swim north, keeping the wall to your right. You'll note that you're heading directly toward a pronounced corner of the wall, which runs perfectly straight until then. At this corner, the wall becomes first a steep cliff and then a rocky promontory with a summit at about 100 feet (30 meters).

Benthic life is clearly prolific here, benefiting from the currents that

A. Here is the characteristic little grotto you'll find at the end of the suggested dive.

B. A gigantic Mithrax *crab moves among the corals by night, a common sight in the darkness.*

C. Two cardinalfish seem unperturbed by the stinging power of an anemone.

D. A large gorgonian below one of the numerous overhangs in the wall at Que Brada.

spectacular, festooned with gorgonians of every type, especially in the area near the drop-off. On the other side, the gorgonians make way for broad patches of white sand. There are at least two large, especially spectacular colonies of yellow tube sponges, and you may well see a small, friendly turtle, often in the company of colorful angelfish. When you get below the boat, there's a good chance that you'll find a dense school of jacks, hovering motionless against the mild current.

become more powerful in this area. You'll find beautiful sponges and gorgonians of every type. Below you, the sandy floor begins to rise, and you can see it heading clearly upward past the corner of the wall. Now head approximately east, continuing to follow the wall and keeping it to your right after the corner. Here, you'll find a number of horizontal crevices, within which you may find gigantic lobsters.

By now, some time will have passed since you entered the water, so you should ascend along the sandy slope, aiming for a rather wide crack that you can see before you. Across from

the large crevice, several stony coral rocks teeming with life deserve careful exploration. The maximum depth at this point is about 65 feet (20 meters), so you should have all the time you need to take things slowly. When you enter the crack, you'll discover that it is actually an extremely complex area, full of little grottoes and recesses that make fabulous photos.

Proceeding along the main crack, you'll come to a plateau at a depth of about 50 feet (15 meters). The *Wave Dancer* is moored off to your right, and your dive is almost complete. Don't forget to save a little air to explore the plateau, which is truly

E. Demonstrating the struggle for space, tube sponges rise from a stony coral.

F. Large sponges develop where the wall abruptly changes direction, constituting a sort of promontory jutting out to sea.

G. By night, a large basket star splays its thousand arms in search of food.

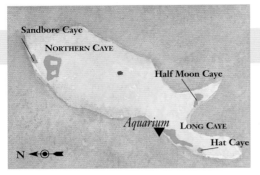

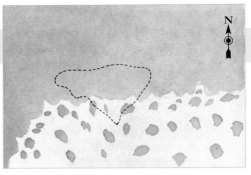

A. A colony of sponges grows over a stony coral on the coral plateau across from the impressive wall at Aquarium.

B. The plateau at Aquarium is so extensive and rich that distracted divers may be tempted to end their exploration here, completely forgetting the wall.

A

B

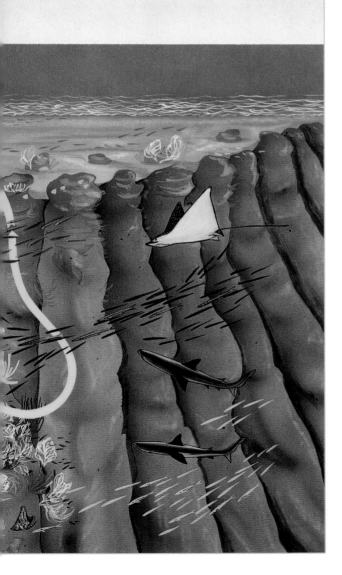

Aquarium
Lighthouse Reef

It's impossible to ignore personal preferences when discussing dive sites. If we had to name our favorite diving area around Belize, we'd definitely choose Aquarium, on the western side of Lighthouse Reef, near the northern tip of Long Caye. At that point, after running north-south for several miles in a more or less straight line, the outer wall of the reef that delimits the atoll gradually shifts to an east-west course. This shift in direction becomes sharper near the buoy marking the Aquarium diving area. You'll find yourself in a corner of the reef where the slope and wall clearly change course, interrupting the regular flow of the currents. When you dive at Aquarium, you'll be exploring the section of wall running east-west near the corner.

As you leave the boat, head north and swim to the coral plateau with its luxuriant life. You'll soon reach the impressive slope, which begins an immense, seemingly endless wall plunging down into the crystal clear water. Let yourself go, but note that the wall is not smooth and compact, but rather rough, with protruding shapes resembling stubby promontories reaching out to the open sea. Here is

A. Two almost completely spherical stony corals prosper on the coral plateau several feet deep.

B. An encounter with passing fish like these jacks is one of the highlights of a dive at Aquarium.

C. A detail of the head of a small squid discovered during a night dive.

D. This tiny arrow blenny (Lucaya-blennius zingaro)—no more than 1.5 inches (4 centimeters) long—lives near the sea floor.

where you'll see most of the benthic creatures in this area.

On this crest, you'll see dense forests of enormous sea fans, broken only intermittently by large, colorful sponges. The yellow organ-pipe sponges are especially spectacular. Along the wall of Aquarium, the current will determine what direction you should follow, but as you are in one of the few diving areas in these waters where the current can become truly powerful, be careful! The myriad of bottom-dwelling creatures is not the only feature that makes a dive in this area interesting and unusual; you're also likely to encounter large pelagic creatures. Eagle rays are quite common, as well as schools of jacks and great, solitary barracudas.

If you descend deeper and look off into the blue depths, you may well see numerous gray sharks. Keep a close eye on your watch and depth gauge while diving at Aquarium, as the unusual shape of the wall, the great depths you can reach, and the clear water can cause significant errors in calculation. Don't forget to spend some time on the coral platform nearer the surface, where you may see great pelagic species.

Aquarium clearly owes its name to its wealth of species, both in its depths and just feet from the surface, where you can spend an entire dive watching beautiful gray angelfish.

E. A small grouper, annoyed by the divers, slowly moves away.

F. A small sponge with a rather singular shape.

G. Right in the middle of the impressive wall, indisputably one of the loveliest anywhere in Belize.

F

G

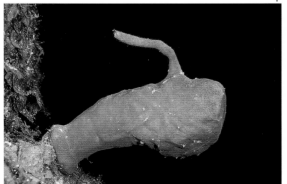

A. A group of colorful sponges that seem to have been the inspiration for the name of this dive.

B. By night, it's a real pleasure to photograph tarpon hunting under the boat. These fish can be as much as 6.5 feet (2 meters) long.

Painted Wall
Lighthouse Reef

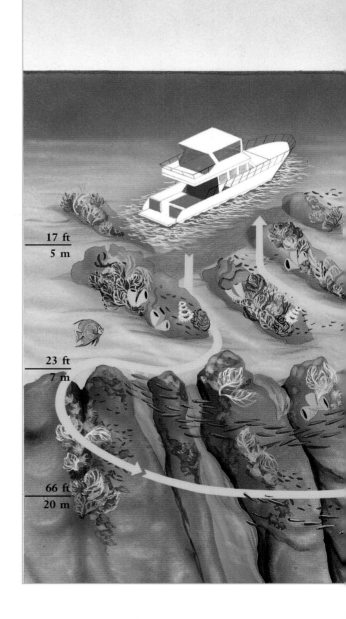

17 ft
5 m

23 ft
7 m

66 ft
20 m

At Painted Wall, north of the northern tip of Long Caye, after running north to south for miles, the western side of the great Lighthouse Atoll makes a wide loop to the east and turns sharply westward again. This section of reef, running east to west, creates a stretch of truly splendid shallow seabeds with an abundance of life, before the reef drops, forming a beautiful wall that reaches the sea floor hundreds of feet farther down.

This shallow area, its depth ranging from 17 to 23 feet (5 to 7 meters), is so beautiful that many divers forget to explore the equally impressive wall. If you came on a live-aboard, the first thing you'll see is a dense school of yellow jacks floating motionless against the current in the shadow of the hull, then the aggressive silhouettes of two or three barracudas, who are always in pursuit of yellowtail snappers.

The sunlight creates fantastic patterns as it passes through tangles of gorgonians and bounces off patches of white sand, spattering the sea floor with a thousand reflections. Stony corals are abundant and diverse, but usually massive, like brain corals. Some are characteristic of the Caribbean—perfectly spherical, about

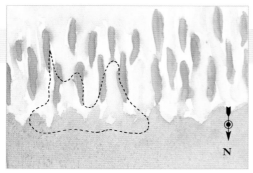

Sandbore Caye

NORTHERN CAYE

Half Moon Caye

Painted Wall

LONG CAYE

Hat Caye

N

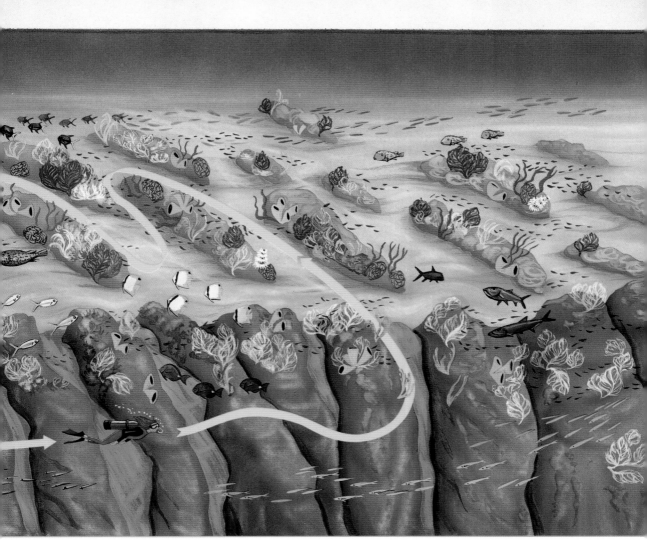

A

B

the size of a soccer ball, and almost always decorated by one or two Christmas tree slugs.

The greatest beauty of the coral reef, however, apart from the showy spectacle of the rich, luminous environment immersed in the clear, deep blue water, is the myriad of fish that populate it; silver or brightly colored, attempting to camouflage themselves or doing their best to show off. A profusion of butterflyfish swims among the rocks; you'll spot

three different species, each swimming in pairs. There are also angelfish, yellow grunts, blue surgeonfish, and parrotfish in every color. You'll see smooth trunkfish, awkward and bulky, porcupine fish, and pufferfish. Shy Nassau groupers and tiger groupers hide among the rocks, while the electric

blue chromis and bicolor violet-and-yellow damselfish make absolutely no effort to conceal themselves.

A few yards north of the *Wave Dancer*'s mooring is a cleaning station, an isolated coral cone a couple of yards tall, rising from the sandy floor of a channel between two low stony

C

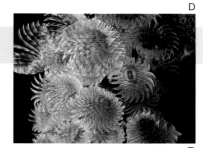

A. A delicate colony of tunicates grows on a red sponge.

B. In the foreground, a barracuda on the coral plateau.

C. The sponges so abundant in the Caribbean may take on the most bizarre shapes, like this colony of Agelas sp.

D. A colorful colony of fan worms (Notaulax sp.), very common annelids in the Caribbean

E. This little blackcap basslet (Gramma melacara) seems hostile to the scuba diver, even though it is no more than 2 inches (5 centimeters) long.

coral ridges. Here, a pair of large Spanish hogfish and a number of small wrasses work ceaselessly to remove parasites from larger fish. Bermuda chub and big blue parrotfish patiently wait their turn—so many fish that they can be seen from quite a distance.

If you're on the plateau when evening falls, your dive will be truly magical. First, the predators approach—large jacks, barracudas, and silvery tarpons. Then the powerful lights of the boat attract a myriad of tiny silversides, their favorite prey. So dive in and stand motionless, with your flashlight off, under the luminous cone of light from the *Wave Dancer*'s headlights. You'll be surrounded by dozens of gigantic tarpon who swim elegantly between light and shadow, launching lightning attacks on their prey, producing a smacking sound with their tails as they turn sharply. Agile jacks swim incessantly around these gigantic predators, while the barracudas hover motionless in shadowy areas, pouncing quickly on any unaware passing fish.

So far, we've only mentioned the coral plateau and what you can see on it by day or night. It's enough for an entire afternoon and evening moored in the same place, if you're on a live-aboard. But the wall is one of the most beautiful in the area, too. To reach it, you'll need to sail north from the mooring site to a drop-off. Depending on the current, you can start your dive by swimming either east or west.

F. By night, the light of the boat on the sea floor attracts clouds of fish and crustaceans, who soon end up in the bellies of voracious tarpon.

G. A colony of sea blades (Pterogorgia sp.) and a red sponge protrude from the coral wall.

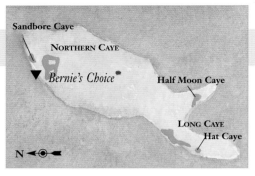

Sandbore Caye
NORTHERN CAYE
▼ *Bernie's Choice*
Half Moon Caye
LONG CAYE
Hat Caye
N

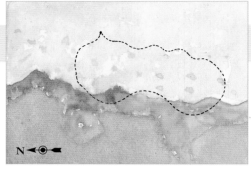

N

A. A good picture of the complexity of a sponge's wall structure. Water flows through the wall, while suspended nutrients are filtered and retained.

B. A small snapper hovers motionless below the base of a gorgonian.

A

B

Bernie's Choice
Lighthouse Reef

26 ft
8 m

66 ft
20 m

100 ft
30 m

This is another beautiful dive near the Lighthouse Reef resort. From the pass that leads you out of the atoll, head south to the buoy that marks the diving area. The seabed, which is flat but extremely rough, is 25 feet (8 meters) below. As usual, there is an abundance of the sea feathers (*Pseudoptergorgia* sp.) so characteristic of the Caribbean.

Toward the open sea, you will find the slope exactly 30 feet (9 meters) away, with the sandy sea floor about 30 feet (9 meters) below you. This flat area, devoid of coral, drops rather abruptly. Descend until you reach a depth of 65 feet (20 meters), then keep the bank to your right. You'll immediately see your first destination in the clear water: a rocky spur that extends straight out from the slope, running toward the open sea. This coral promontory first interrupts the profile of the bank, then joins a ridge similar to the hull of an overturned boat. Swim to the nearest section.

The first interesting area to explore is where the rock approaches the sandy sea floor, creating a drop of about 6.5 feet (2 meters). Many branching sponges hang from the vault, glowing bright red when you shine your flashlight on them. The white sand of the

sea floor reflects the sunlight, beautifully illuminating the interior of this recess. You are about 100 feet (30 meters) deep here. Move out a little from where the wall touches the sand to where it briefly flattens, forming the hull-shaped structure noted above.

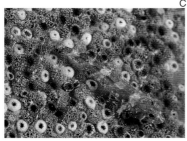

The top of the hull has a wealth of life, much more than the surrounding sea floor, due to its exposure to the current. Here, more than anywhere else, you may see eagle rays, solitary barracudas, and small schools of yellow jacks. Spend a little time in this place, but don't dwell too long. Most importantly, don't succumb to the temptation to descend deeper, as this would make it impossible to reach your second destination.

Continue exploring beyond the ridge you have just examined to another detrital cone. You'll soon reach a structure similar to the first one, but more like a child's drawing of a mountain. This varied and complex rocky formation juts out into the open

sea. On the peak, at about 65 feet (20 meters), you will see several large stony corals, then some brightly colored sponges. The northern side ahead of you descends to a wide, flat, sandy sea floor dotted with isolated stony corals and sea fans and edged by another rocky promontory, which you can glimpse in the distance.

Of special note is the large yellow organ-pipe sponge—it has at least twenty different pipes, all more than 2 feet (60 centimeters) long. When you come to this sponge, it's time to head toward the boat. Go up the channel, which is marked by the base of the yellow sponge, then turn right and swim to a depth of about 30 feet (9 meters), to a plateau populated by gorgonians.

A. The large sponges in the foreground and the shape of a diver in the distance give you an idea of the enormity of this beautiful wall.

B. A tiny crinoid climbs up the branch of a red gorgonian.

C. A small blenny (Enneanectes atrorus) characteristic of Lighthouse Reef.

D. A trumpetfish (Aulostomus maculatus) tries to camouflage itself in the branches of a gorgonian.

E. Small turtles are a common sight in these waters.

F. Tube sponges grow below the branches of a gorgonian, at a depth of about 100 feet (30 meters).

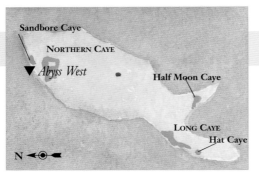

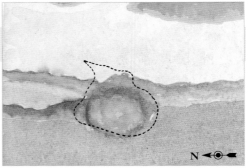

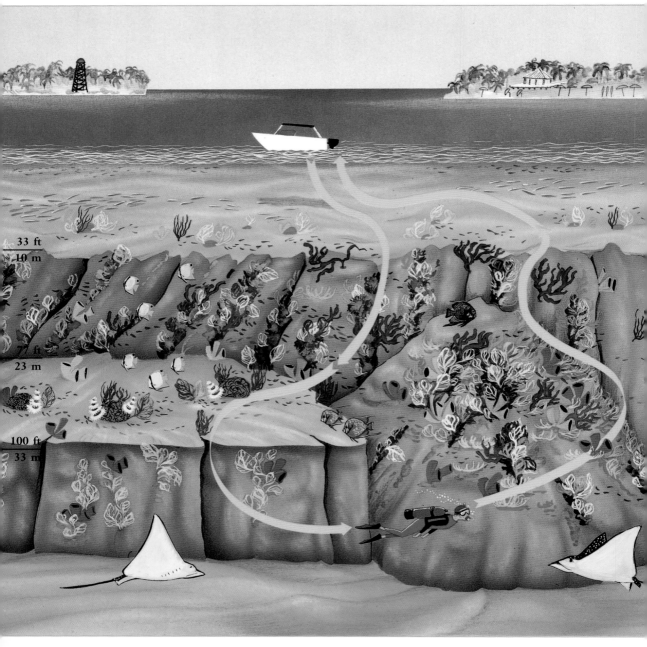

33 ft
10 m

77 ft
23 m

100 ft
33 m

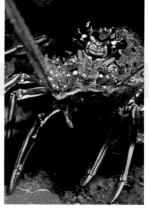

A. An image of the large, comfortable resort at Lighthouse Reef.

B. Peeping out of its den, a beautiful lobster uses its antennae in an attempt to investigate the intrusion.

A

B

Abyss West
Lighthouse Reef

This is the northern tip of Lighthouse Reef. Here, about a mile apart, are two sandy islets covered with vegetation: Sandbore Caye and Northern Caye. The first is quite tiny, the northernmost emerged land in the atoll, and is very close to the northern end of the coral reef—hence the lighthouse. The other islet, which is much larger—a couple of miles in diameter—has several brackish marshes, and is home to a small but lovely resort, with a landing strip for vacation flights that connect the island with Belize City. Live-aboards usually don't come here, nor do dive operators from the mainland, so the best way to reach this area is to stay right at Lighthouse Reef.

It's just a few minutes by boat from Lighthouse Reef to the diving area, where you'll moor at a fixed buoy right across from the main island. Below, the reef runs northeast to southwest. This is also the direction you should follow during your dive. Descend onto the sea floor 30 feet (9 meters) below the boat. It is flat, with small stony corals alternating with beautiful gorgonians, sea feathers (*Pseudopterogorgia* sp.) and broad patches of white sand. Follow the rough surface that gently slopes out to sea, ornamented

A   B   C

F

A. Yet another example of two sponges competing for space.

B. Examples of blackcap basslets (Gramma melacara) can be found everywhere along the wall at depths below 65 feet (20 meters).

by sponges and gorgonians and populated by a number of reef fish.

If you want to follow the dive plan suggested here, continue out toward the open sea. At a depth of about 75 feet (23 meters), the slope levels to a broad patch of coral sand. If the water is murky, you may think you've reached the bottom, but as you continue out to sea, the depth increases. You'll finally reach a depth of 90 to 110 feet (27 to 33 meters), passing a distinctive coral structure to your left that rises about 50 feet (15 meters) from the sandy area. Between 90 to 110 feet (27 and 33 meters), you'll see a drop-off where the reef plunges rapidly, and seemingly endlessly, with no sight of a flat floor. This steep slope, sometimes nearly a wall, is truly beautiful to

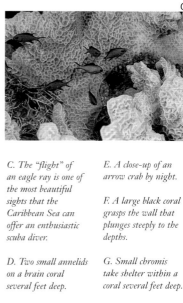

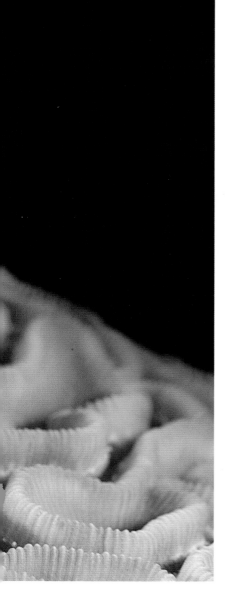

D

E

C. The "flight" of an eagle ray is one of the most beautiful sights that the Caribbean Sea can offer an enthusiastic scuba diver.

E. A close-up of an arrow crab by night.

F. A large black coral grasps the wall that plunges steeply to the depths.

D. Two small annelids on a brain coral several feet deep.

G. Small chromis take shelter within a coral several feet deep.

explore, a garden of gorgonians and sponges, with a wealth of pelagic fish such as solitary tunas or eagle rays.

To avoid going too deep, head toward the southwest. You will soon leave the drop-off behind you, while the tower you previously passed to your left will rise over your head, leading you to the middle of the wall at a depth of about 100 feet (30 meters). Continue your exploration by steadily decreasing your depth, until you are on top of the rise at 50 feet (15 meters). From here, heading east, you can easily return to the gentle slope where you started, and then to the boat.

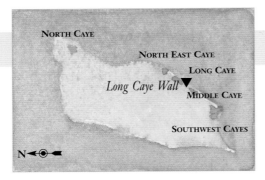

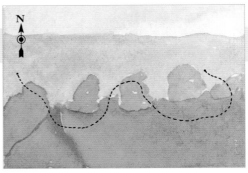

17 ft
5 m

50 ft
15 m

A. *A small fish seems lost in this coral labyrinth.*

B. *Another example of the richness of the walls near Belize. This is over 100 feet (30 meters) deep, and the sponges are truly large and colorful.*

A

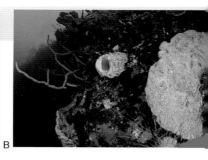

B

Long Caye Wall
Glover's Reef

There is a lovely diving area just south of the small islet known as Long Caye. As is often the case at Turneffe Islands and Lighthouse Reef atolls, the most beautiful dives are where the regular line of the reef breaks off and changes direction, and where the reef itself faces south. Both of these conditions are met here.

Long Caye Wall is aptly named, as it certainly involves an exploration of a large and impressive wall, but uniquely the site is also fine for snorkeling. In fact, the wall can even be reached by swimming out from the island's beach. If you want to do some snorkeling or are planning a dive from the land, be sure to enter the water at the side of the islet farthest to the east. Entering the water is not easy, especially if the sea is a little rough, due to the abundance of vigorous corals even in the first few feet of water. You'll find many types of coral, but watch out for the fire corals, which are especially common here and can cause burning rashes if touched. In any event, you will be far better off in a boat.

Beyond the shallow, coral-rich seabed, where snorkelers can see dense schools of parrotfish, angelfish, and

A

cross it using one of the crevices that fracture it, descend along the wall. It drops gradually, leaving large, luminous bare patches of white sand interspersed with areas covered by a myriad of sponges, spectacular branches of black corals and whip corals, and beautiful, isolated gorgonians. The organisms of the benthic world are not the only attraction here—this area also has an abundance of pelagic fish passing through, and you may see spectacular creatures like eagle rays, barracudas, and occasional isolated stingrays. Once again, in a dive of this type,

other denizens of the coral kingdom, is a vast area of light sand. Here black stingrays bury themselves under the sediment, and the trails of a myriad of conches are easy to spot. A profusion of garden eels poke out of the sedimentary seabed, ready to dart back into their holes at the slightest sign of danger. The sandy floor stretches for dozens of yards, while you descend to a depth of about 40 feet (12 meters), before a coral ridge rises before you. This topography is characteristic of the sea floor around Belize, where the reef divides the sand from the outer wall. The corals rise 20 feet (6 meters) from the seabed, with thousands upon thousands of life forms. You'll find large corals and a profusion of gorgonians that offer shelter to fish of every kind, often in search of cleaner fish or shrimp. There are also large sponges in a wide variety of forms, with colors ranging from yellow to brown. Between the sand and the coral ridge are numerous large boulders teeming with life. As you pass over the coral structure, or

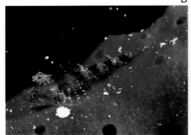

B

C

it is easiest to descend to the maximum planned depth, then gradually ascend, exploring the seabed, until you reach the spectacular coral ridge and the peaceful sandy region.

D

A. This small blenny seems to watch the photographer curiously.

B. A small blackedge triplefin (Enneanectes atrorus) is well camouflaged on a red sponge.

C. During the day, an arrow crab takes shelter within a sponge.

D. The cracks in the coral that lead to the vertical walls are truly quite spectacular and full of life.

E. A Niphates sp. sponge climbs up a round stony coral.

A. A beautiful group of various species of gorgonians: Pterogorgia *sp. in* the background and Gorgonia flabellum in the foreground.

B. Two types of sponges, whose branches intertwine on the coral floor several feet deep.

Gorgonia Gallery
Glover's Reef

This dive is located in the southern zone of Glover's Reef, near the two islets known as the Southwest Cayes. One of them is home to the Manta Resort vacation village, which is completely dedicated to the underwater exploration of Glover's, while the other is private. The section of sea floor you'll be exploring faces south and first runs due west-east, then curves to run approximately northeast.

The scene from the boat is truly magnificent; on the crystalline water of a lagoon with a white sand floor you float between the deep blue ocean and the green palms growing on the two islands. Jump into the water, where you'll find yourself on a sandy sea floor between 23 and 33 feet (7 and 10 meters) deep. Swim east to find the coral wall. You can also swim south, following the wall from west to east, then continuing along the section heading northeast, but you run the risk of having to swim right into the northern current that is more prevalent in this area. So swim to the west for a hundred feet or so, until you reach the first masses of coral that rise several feet from the sand. In a flash, you'll understand why this is called Gorgonia Gallery. Gorgonians

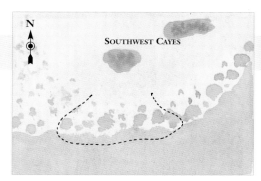

SOUTHWEST CAYES

N

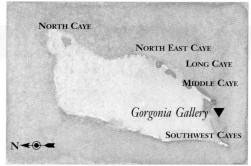

NORTH CAYE

NORTH EAST CAYE
LONG CAYE
MIDDLE CAYE

Gorgonia Gallery ▼

SOUTHWEST CAYES

N

23 ft
7 m

33 ft
10 m

40 ft
12 m

A

B

C

D

A. Below 65 feet
(20 meters), the
seabed becomes richer
and more colorful.
Thick coral masses
never fail to attract
attention.

B. The lens captures
a small crab from the
genus Pelia on the
wall of a sponge.

C. A snapper moves
among the corals in
the shallow part of
the reef.

D. A beautiful
colony of Aplysina
cauliformis *frames
the scuba diver's
silhouette.*

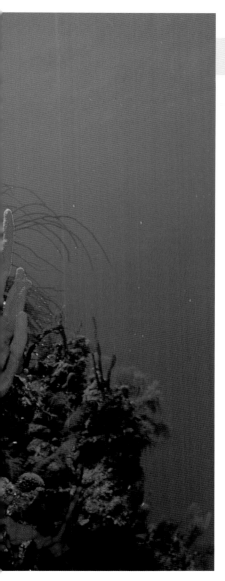

E. The deeper part of the wall is full of deep-water sea fans (Iciligorgia *sp.*).

F. At night, this small squirrelfish finds shelter in a crevice among the corals.

are more abundant here than in almost any other place in the Caribbean Sea.

The coral rocks are very complex and jagged, rising over a flat, sandy seabed before falling rapidly on the opposite side. But don't expect a sheer wall; though the seabed does drop steeply in places, it never becomes vertical. Large expanses of hard corals, always embellished with great gorgonian fans or colorful sponges, alternate with broad patches of white sand, making this area, which already has a southern exposure, especially luminous. In addition to bottom dwellers, it's not uncommon to also see pelagic fish. Of course the presence of any particular fish is unpredictable in any diving area, but reef fish— parrotfish, triggerfish, surgeonfish, snappers, and angelfish—are always abundant. Jacks and barracudas (both solitary and sometimes in small schools) are not at all uncommon.

Enjoy this beautiful part of the sea floor, keeping the slope to your right. During the first few minutes of the dive, move northeast to southwest; then, following the profile of the reef, swim due west. When the no-decompression limit on the dive computer begins to drop significantly, gradually decrease your depth until you again find yourself near the stony corals, then the sandy flat area, and finally to the boat moored close by.

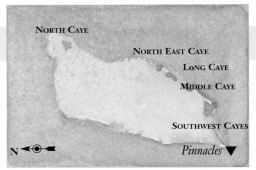

NORTH CAYE

NORTH EAST CAYE

LONG CAYE

MIDDLE CAYE

SOUTHWEST CAYES

Pinnacles ▼

N

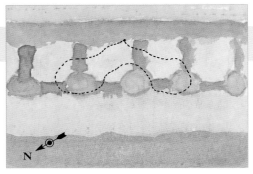

N

A. A Bermuda chub enjoys the services of a small cleaner fish, Bodianus pulchellus.

B. Along the beautiful wall at Pinnacles, an enormous vase sponge is decorated by a red arborescent sponge.

A

B

Pinnacles
Glover's Reef

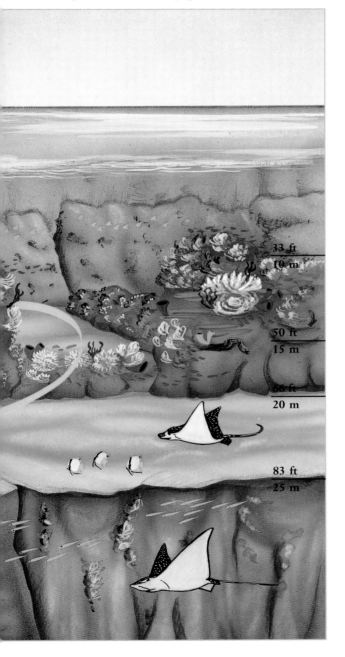

33 ft
10 m

50 ft
15 m

66 ft
20 m

83 ft
25 m

The southernmost reef, Glover's is also the most isolated of the three. Six tiny cayes emerge from the waters of the splendid coral lagoon, some with excellent small resorts that offer diving opportunities in the area. These are probably the most pristine, well-preserved seabeds in all of Belize. Practically the only divers here are those who stay at the resorts scattered throughout the atoll—only a handful of boats come here from continental Belize—so tourism is anything but dominant.

While doing our research, we discovered that this gorgeous area of the barrier reef is known by at least two different names—Pinnacle and Cathedral Spires are used interchangeably. It is in the southernmost part of Glover's, where the coral reef that runs from north-northeast to south-southwest turns a sharp corner, shifting west to east. As the prevailing currents generally come from the north, this area is full of life and color. But what's unique about it is not so much the creatures that live on its coral buttresses as its spectacular morphology. Although currents sweep past the reef, this area is quite sheltered from prevailing winds, so the sea is usually calm.

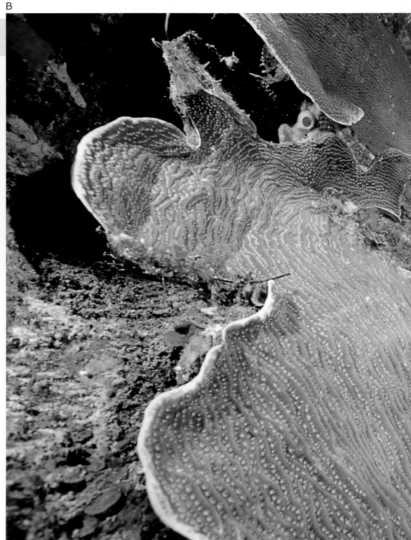

Coming from one of the little sandy islands, circle the tip of the reef and head north for a bit to your immersion point. The reef emerges from the water in this area, completely protecting the interior of the lagoon from the waves. From its exposed peak, the reef slides gently down to form an extensive coral platform at a depth between 25 and 35 feet (8 and 11 meters). Head approximately northwest until you reach the distinctive depressed areas of the sandy floor. These are actually holes opening in the corals; reaching at their deepest a depth of 65 to 85 feet (20 to 26 meters),

C

they curve along parallel to the edge of the reef. These sandy patches are separated by elongated coral structures that rise above the bottom of the hole to within 50 feet (15 meters) of the surface. Similar structures on the side that faces the open sea are broken by the spectacular coral towers that make this dive so distinctive. The towers rise to almost 30 feet (10 meters) and face the coral drop-off, which leads directly to the depths.

After you cross the coral plateau

A. Sea turtles find the coral sand beaches of Caribbean islands to be an ideal place to lay their eggs.

B. A sponge stands out right in the center of a large colony of stony corals.

C. A small blenny seeks refuge from predators within the corals.

D. A close-up of the head of a trumpetfish, an extremely common species in the waters of the Caribbean.

E. The presence of so many fish in one place indicates a cleaning station.

and the sandy patches, you'll have to decide whether to swim south, exploring the coral towers one by one, or to descend along the steep slope and explore greater depths, so you should quickly cross the shallow areas, descend for a few minutes along the slope, populated by fish, colorful sponges, and gorgonians, and then climb back up to explore the bold pinnacles one by one, finally coming back to the coral plateau and slowly returning to the boat.

B

C

A. Cayos Cochinos is
a little group of islets
halfway between
the larger islands of
the Bay Islands
archipelago and
continental Honduras.

B. Any trip to
Honduras should
include a visit to the
magnificent ruins of
Maya di Copan in the
country's interior.

INTRODUCTION
Honduras

Diving in Honduras really means diving around the Bay Islands, a group of islands off the Honduran coast. The coast of Honduras runs west to east; the country borders Belize, Nicaragua, and Guatemala and El Salvador inland. The sea near the coast is not good for diving due to the enormous amount of silt discharged into the sea by rivers.

The first islands you see toward the north belong to Cayos Cochinos, a small group of eleven rocky or coral islets grouped around the largest one, Cochino Grande, and surrounded by a coral reef. The most remote area within the Bay Islands archipelago, Cayos Cochinos is rarely visited by divers and tourists, both because of the distance from the main islands and because the water is generally less clear than the other islands, even though it is full of bizarre, truly surprising creatures for macrophotographers.

Then come the larger islands, generally aligned from southwest to northeast. The southernmost island is Utila, then Roatan, the largest island, tiny Barbareta, and finally Guanaja. Utila, Roatan, and Guanaja are perfect for diving. Utila is a little more economical, making it attractive to young people, many of whom come here to take scuba diving lessons. Lovely Roatan offers lodgings for every pocketbook, picturesque local villages, magnificent beaches, and a myriad of diving areas. Remote Guanaja appeals to more solitary tastes, and has recently been connected to the other islands by a new, efficient airport. All

the islands offer magnificent diving, rich seabeds, and crystalline waters.

Roatan certainly has the most variety, due primarily to its larger size and consequently larger coral reef. In our opinion, the rumor that the northern side offers more beautiful

sea floors than the southern side is absolutely not true. In fact, we recommend organizing your trip so that you spend equal time diving on both sides.

The most classic diving area on the southern coast of Roatan, Mary's Place, is extremely beautiful, and always has sharks off the southern coast. To the north, underwater encounters with dolphins in semi-captivity can be organized. The two shipwrecks off Roatan, one to the north and one to the south, are a joy for divers. Another sunken ship worth exploring is the wreck of the *Jado Trader*, off Guanaja.

C. A small fishing village right on the beach of one of the Cayos Cochinos islets. Life is simple here, and inhabitants go out fishing in wooden pirogues.

D. The West End Bay beach on the southwest tip of Roatan is one of the island's most beautiful and popular beaches.

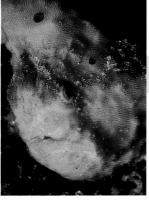

A

B

Toon Town
Cayos Cochinos

A little group of islets set off from the rest of the Bay Islands, Cayos Cochinos are the closest islands to the Honduran coast, and thus suffer most from the influence of the rivers that cloud the water with their silt. Nevertheless, you should by no means eliminate Cayos Cochinos from your exploration of the Bay Islands seabeds.

First of all, these islands have very picturesque villages, inhabited for the most part by friendly local fishermen who still use traditional pirogues equipped with sails. Second, the water is not always murky. Finally, dives here will reveal truly unique, amazing, often once-in-a-lifetime encounters with bizarre little creatures. Of course, macrophotography fans will especially enjoy this kind of dive, but probably everyone will have fun discovering these bizarre creatures.

The dive suggested here—certainly not the only one possible along the coast of Cayos Cochinos—runs along the northwest coast of Cochino Grande, the largest islet in the little archipelago. It's a distinctive dive, not only because of the creatures you'll find here but also because it's a descent over a seabed that is not shaped by coral. Instead, you'll be swimming

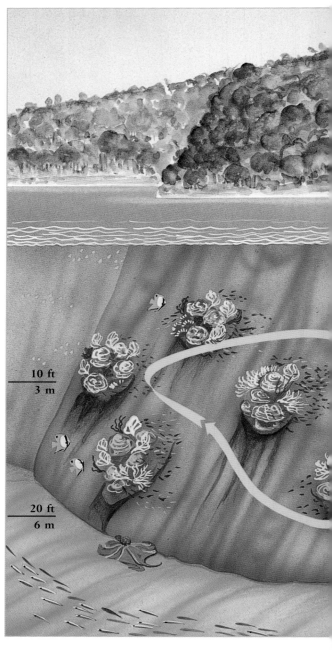

10 ft
3 m

20 ft
6 m

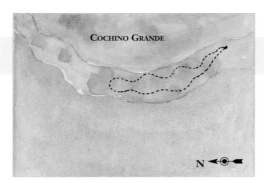

COCHINO GRANDE

N

Toon Town

COCHINO GRANDE

COCHINO PEQUEÑO

N

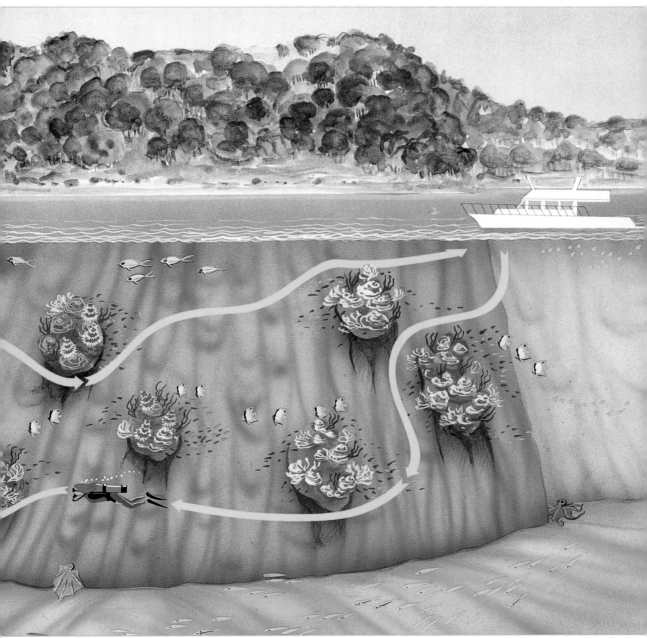

A

over the geological topography of the island, which extends underwater. While it is colonized by corals of various types, they nevertheless do not change the general morphology.

The best advice is to take the opportunity of a fabulous night dive. It's not that there are any fewer creatures during the day, but at night you can use your flashlight to focus on a small area, where you can closely examine the strange, colorful life forms that populate it. This will afford you a much better look at creatures that would probably blend into the

B

C

A. A large Astrospartus *extends its arms during the night. It is an extremely common sight in the shallow waters of Toon Town.*

B. Even nudibranchs are common among the rocks of the steep sea floor at Toon Town. This is a Phyllodesmium *sp. gastropod.*

D

E

sea's general blue light during the day and be easy to miss.

The boat usually moors in a little inlet about halfway up the western coast of the island. The northernmost point of the bay is where your dive will begin. You'll find yourself swimming along a very jagged, steep slope. Head north throughout the dive, keeping the wall to your right as you gradually decrease your depth and return, maintaining a depth of 10 to 20 feet (3 to 6 meters).

What's so special awaiting you among the rocks in this wall? In just one dive at a very shallow depth, we saw many examples of basket stars (*Astrophyton muricatum*) that open

only at dusk, while a large octopus hunted small fish not far off. A long-snout seahorse (*Hypocampus reidi*) coiled its tail around a gorgonian with white branches. Difficult to see at night, its bright color stood out on the white branches. Below a sponge, a few yards from each other, two toadfish, one completely yellow and one black, waved the antennae on their heads,

C. A goby timidly peeps out from a red sponge.

D. A brain coral hosts two elegant annelids.

E. A tiny crab from the genus Padochela *climbs up a gorgonian.*

F. Another contender for the "most ugly" award, Batrachoides gilberti *is quite common in the crevices, and can often be seen at night.*

F

A. During the night,
an octopus hunts on
the sea floor, spreading
its tentacles and
mantle over its prey.

B. A small slipper
lobster (Parribacus
antarticus) warily
leaves its den during
the night.

C. Two aggressive
blennies poke out of the
entries to their dens.

B

C

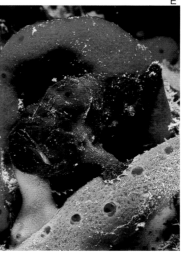

equipped with a decoy to lure small prey toward their disproportionately large mouths. We observed a large number of oddly shaped nudibranchs, gigantic crabs wandering among the corals, shrimp perched among the gorgonian branches, and many small tube worms that looked like Christmas trees.

But the award for oddest creature definitely goes to a *Batracoides giliberti* that we discovered camouflaged inside its den. This toadfish, its large mouth bristling with appendages, lies immobile on the sea floor all day long, waiting for prey to pass within striking distance. This typical Caribbean fish will make a valuable addition to the collections of underwater photographers.

D, E. Two toadfish, yellow and black, lie motionless on their paw-shaped fins, just a few inches from each other. Their antennae have a protuberance above the mouth that acts as a decoy.

F. A splendid seahorse grasping a gorgonian branch with its tail.

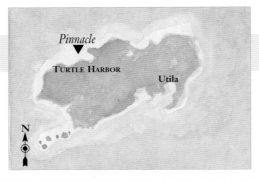

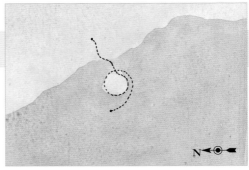

A. In deep water, large sponges colonize the walls at Pinnacle.

B. The polyps of this gorgonian are filtering the water, rich in nourishment, at Pinnacle.

A

B

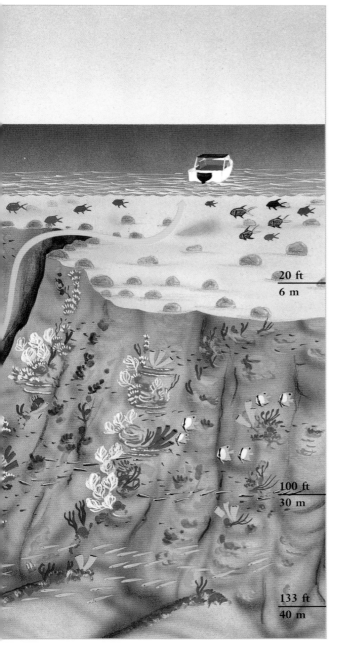

20 ft
6 m

100 ft
30 m

133 ft
40 m

Pinnacle
Utila

Pinnacle, in the nature reserve on the northern coast of Utila, is certainly one of the island's most distinctive dives. Here, as is typical of Caribbean sea floors, the coral wall descends sharply and quickly from the shallow waters on the plaform, leveling out at about 130 feet (39 meters). The difference from other diving areas is that here a coral pinnacle rises from the seabed not far from the wall and the flat floor to about 20 feet (6 meters) from the surface. The side that faces the main reef ends on a saddle only 100 feet (30 meters) deep.

Of course, the spectacular morphology of the sea floor alone—which is set off by the clear water—makes this dive worthwhile. Also consider that the pinnacle projecting from the coastal wall acts as a magnet for various species of fish, who move through here in schools. The current also has a strong effect on the two walls facing each other, which boast a true abundance of spectacular benthic life.

Normally, you should jump in the water right over the top of the pointed rock. You'll be about 20 feet (6 meters) deep, and the top reef is just barely 30 feet (9 meters) in

A

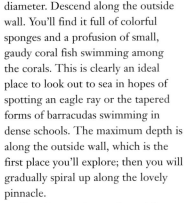

E

B

diameter. Descend along the outside wall. You'll find it full of colorful sponges and a profusion of small, gaudy coral fish swimming among the corals. This is clearly an ideal place to look out to sea in hopes of spotting an eagle ray or the tapered forms of barracudas swimming in dense schools. The maximum depth is along the outside wall, which is the first place you'll explore; then you will gradually spiral up along the lovely pinnacle.

Spend some time at the saddle between the main wall and the inner side of the pinnacle. You'll find it to be extremely rich and colorful. As you ascend, both atop the peak and in the channel, a school of jacks or barracudas will likely show up, attracted by the bubbles. Swim out into the blue depths from the wall of the reef and cross the approximately 65 feet (20 meters) that separate you from the main wall, then come to the top of the plateau at about 13 feet (4 meters), where you can peacefully complete your precautionary decompression.

*A., B. At the base of the wall, pink and white vase sponges (*Callyspongia *sp.) offer interesting photo opportunities.*

C. A small blenny vanishes in the labyrinth of a brain coral, at a depth of several feet.

*D. At night, if you shine a light on the gorgonians, you will find a multitude of tiny mimetic crabs (*Pelia *sp.).*

E. On our ascent, we see a beautiful angelfish near a gorgonian branch.

C

D

Don't forget that in summer, great whale sharks pass by off the north coast of Utila. So as soon as you get back into the boat, don't forget to look out to sea. If you spot a group of birds circling over the area, and if the water is boiling with foam, it's likely the site of a mass of plankton being attacked by fish—and whale sharks. Meanwhile, birds take the opportunity to hunt sardines, who themselves give chase to plankton.

F. A tuft of white
annelids protrudes
from a stony coral.

G. You're almost
certain to find a school
of resident jacks in the
waters of Pinnacle.

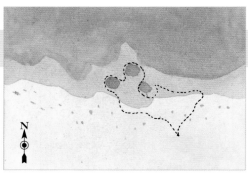

A. This photo reveals the richness of the underwater walls at Utila, with a wealth of sponges and gorgonians.

B. A lovely colony of spectacular pillar coral several feet deep.

A

B

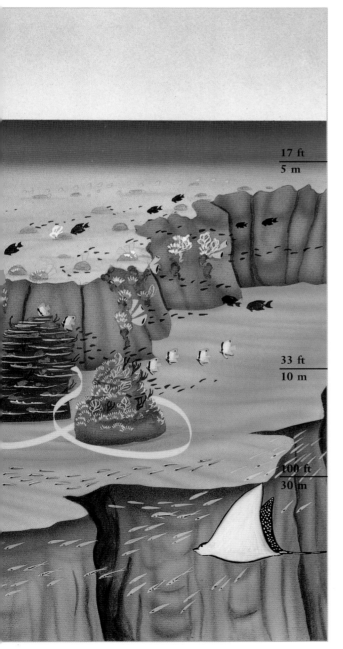

17 ft
5 m

33 ft
10 m

100 ft
30 m

Blackish Point
Utila

This is one of the most beautiful dives on the northern coast of Utila. It is a classic wall dive, extremely impressive, full of encounters with various species of fish, and on a reef with an abundance of hard corals, soft corals, and other invertebrates. The diving point is off a massive promontory that extends northward from the center of the island. The entire promontory area, including the swampy regions on the mainland, are part of the Turtle Harbor Marine Reserve and Wildlife Refuge, created to preserve both the marine environment and the island's delicate marsh ecosystem.

In addition to the marsh environment, the northern coast of Utila immediately west of Blackish Point has a beach where hawksbill turtles often come to lay their eggs after mating in the sea. Of course, this makes an encounter with one of these reptiles more likely here than in other areas along the coast of Utila.

A dive along the reef off the point is rather simple, and suitable for divers of any level of experience. In fact, the reef comes within 15 feet (4.5 meters) of the surface, then plunges vertically down to 100 feet (30 meters), where it meets the sand, then slopes down

C

A

B

A. A beautiful colony of gorgonians (Iciligorgia sp.) at a depth of about 80 feet (24 meters).

B. Sponges crowd each other on a patch of sand, battling for living space.

C. By night, many octopuses wander about the shallower areas of the reef.

D. As you rise from the lower depths, you'll find beautiful colonies of plate corals.

E. These spectacular, delicate tunicates are known as Clavelina puertosecensis.

much farther. The stony coral and hard coral formations in general are vivid and rich. Even the sea floor looks brightly colored, especially in the first several feet, due to the great variety of coral. You'll find many brain corals, pointed pillar corals, and beautiful formations of lettuce coral.

The rich benthic life is not the only marvelous feature of this part of the seabed. The wall is broken by many rather distinct crevices. Seen from above, the slope almost appears to be undulating. At the crevices, the main wall drops only about 17 to 60 feet (5 to 18 meters) rather than to about 100 feet (30 meters) as elsewhere. Beautiful coral towers stand on these intermediate terraces, rising to create spectacular narrow passageways among their sides and the wall of the reef.

Of course, there is a wealth of benthic life on the edges of these waves, where the main wall juts out toward the open sea before returning toward the coast. Because it is exposed to the current and faces the open sea, you may see a large quantity of fish swimming by, especially eagle rays. The pinnacles and stony coral formations are full of squirrelfish, soldierfish, and large green morays. Sometimes you may see a multitude of dark blue soldierfish passing by, intent on feeding among the corals. Another feature makes this place especially popular among divers: the area off this point is where you're most likely to spot passing whale sharks. Especially from December to February, it's not uncommon to see dense flocks of birds circling over the same area. If you approach, you'll see mackerel or other small pelagic fish jumping out of the water, intent on hunting smaller fish, which in their turn are attracted by masses of plankton. This is when you may well spot the great black fin slicing through the water or the enormous mouth of the fish as it emerges briefly. It's one thing to identify a whale shark in the water, but managing to dive near one is altogether more difficult. Still, it's worth a try; the experience would be an unparalleled thrill.

Going back to the beautiful wall of Blackish Point, remember that there is no precise direction to take when starting your dive. Everything depends on whether there is a current or, if the water is still, on your own or your guide's personal preference. Usually, when dive operators organize a trip to Blackish Point, they also include a stop at the splendid cayes south of the island, a true Caribbean paradise.

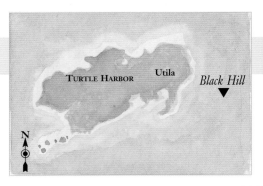

TURTLE HARBOR   Utila

Black Hill ▼

N

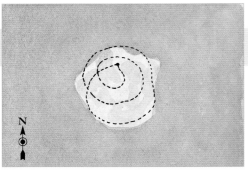

N

A. It is by no means uncommon to see a lone barracuda in the waters of Black Hill.

B. A vase sponge grows over a stony coral at a depth of about 100 feet (30 meters).

A

B

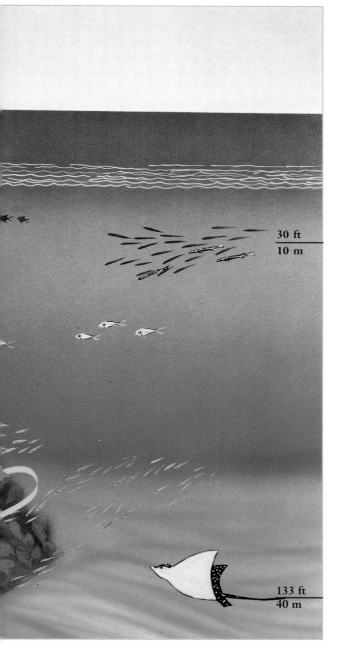

30 ft
10 m

133 ft
40 m

Black Hill
Utila

B lack Hill offers a distinctly unusual dive for the waters off the Bay Islands. Here, however, you'll be exploring a true coral shoal that rises far from the coast from a deep sea floor, without breaking the water's surface.

This dive is located to the east of the island of Utila. The point where you should jump in is some distance out into the open sea, about three miles from the coast and approximately half an hour's boat ride from the village of Utila. As the name implies, it is a hill in the sand about 130 feet (39 meters) deep that rises up to 35 feet (11 meters) from the surface. The base is several hundred feet in diameter, while the summit is flat and about 65 feet (20 meters) around.

The distinctive feature of Black Hill is that it has some of the greatest abundance of fish in the entire archipelago. Of course, a dive that normally offers a wealth of fish could prove to be disappointing, as there's no guarantee that the fish will be there when you come, but still, it generally lives up to its reputation. You'll almost always find a school of sedentary yellow jacks, and it's common to spot many barracudas, either alone or in schools. Sometimes you may encounter little groups of Atlantic spadefish.

A

*A. A school of
yellow jacks crosses
the open sea.*

*B. An example of
Equetus sp., a
wonderful little fish
found in the darkest,
most hidden crevices.*

*C. Yellow branches of
Aplysina sp. sponges
grow on the reef.*

*D. A splendid
corner of the wall:
a large colony of
orange Agelas sp.
sponges entirely covers
the rock, while
Iciligorgia sp.
gorgonian fans rise
from the floor.*

Fish aren't the only feature of this fine diving area, however. As soon as you enter the water, you'll be able to admire lovely fantail and sea plumes. In deeper areas, you may see beautiful green or brown branches of black coral, as well as a variety of sponges. Usually divers use this area for their first dive of the day, both because it's relatively deep and difficult and because for some reason it appears to be easier to spot fish in the morning than in the afternoon.

You should leave the village of Utila early, taking advantage of calm, windless days. The first puzzle is identifying the top of the reef. It isn't always marked by a fixed mooring buoy, as waves and wind often wash the buoy away. Another feature of Black Hill, which is probably the reason for the richness of its life, is the frequent presence of a slight current that usually runs north to south. The current won't disturb your dive; it is rarely strong, and the slopes of the reef always offer shelter and protection to divers. Still, it brings in a large quantity of nutrients for benthic organisms and fish. It can be magnificent to drop onto the reef and watch the motionless school of jacks, snouts pointed into the current.

When you find the summit and finish gearing up, enter the clear

water. You'll immediately be struck by the wealth of gorgonians growing at the top and the contrast they make with the blue of the sea. If you look down, it's not difficult to spot the bottom 130 feet (39 meters) below. The slopes of the reef are not very steep, but you will nevertheless quickly reach the maximum planned depth. Go deeper than 100 feet (30 meters), however, so that you can stop

B

for a minute to stabilize and admire this evocative little underwater mountain rising toward the sun. Even if you decide to cut your descent short, remember that from that point on, your exploration will begin as you spiral back up around the hill, making a perfect multilevel dive.

C

D

*E. Large sponges and
gorgonians grow on
the underwater wall.
The diver in the
background helps set
the right proportions.*

*F. A banded coral
shrimp (Stenophus
sp.) climbs up the wall
of a barrel sponge.*

E

F

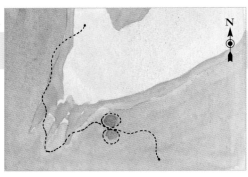

A. This very delicate coral prospers in a beautiful colony in a part of the seabed that is protected from the violence of the waves, which would destroy it.

B. A beautiful branch of red whip coral rises from the floor about 100 feet (30 meters) deep.

A

B

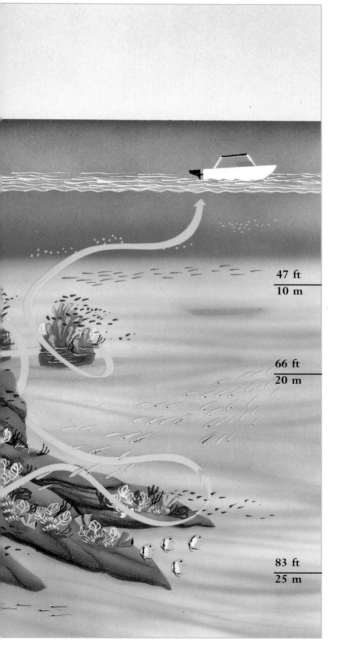

47 ft
10 m

66 ft
20 m

83 ft
25 m

Herbie's Place
Roatan

Herbie's Place is one of the most beautiful dives that the rich and colorful seabeds of Roatan can offer. This dive plan will lead you along the seabeds of the lovely southwest tip of the island, West End Point, just beyond the beautiful beach of West End Bay. The dive is somewhat difficult, as you'll need to jump in from an unanchored boat, drop into the blue depths to the sea floor, and rise back up to the surface in the same manner. Thus, it is quite important to rely on an experienced guide for this dive.

The following description may seem backward, as you'll find yourself descending onto a sea floor, proceeding to the open sea and greater depths, and coming up far from the coast. It does seem more logical to jump in at the end and return toward the coast and shallower depths, but in most cases this dive would be against the current. So it's clear that you should rely on an expert local guide to handle this dive.

The dive starts at the southern coast, just beyond West End Bay. Past the beach, the coast becomes rocky. The descent will begin right at the lighthouse. Jump into the water over 300 feet (100 meters) off the coast, and descend directly onto a seabed

B

C

A. This photo is quite representative of the seabed at Herbie's, where the corals grow on a white sand floor that makes the environment truly luminous.

B. Extensive colonies of pillar coral are characteristic in the shallower areas around Herbie's.

C. A diver examines a beautiful pink sponge.

45 feet (14 meters) deep. As already noted, the current is likely to push you toward the southwest and the open sea. Follow a coral wall below the water that runs in the same direction, as if it were an underwater extension of the island. You'll immediately note how luxuriant this part of the sea is, as you spot forests of gorgonians, large black triggerfish, and dense schools of black surgeonfish.

As you move to the open sea, an encounter with eagle rays becomes more and more likely. Slowly dive to 70 feet (21 meters) and continue in the same direction, pushed by the gentle current, in crystalline water rendered even more luminous by the patches of white sand that cover the sea floor. As you move off into the

blue depths, you'll continue to see schools of fish, including yellow jacks, amberjacks, and Bermuda chub. You'll soon note that the reef is descending slightly and separating into different low coral ridges running subparallel to each other. Follow the main ridge, keeping your depth more or less constant. You'll easily spot a myriad of large lobsters among the coral crevices, and come across turtles engrossed in feeding on organisms that they break off the coral floor with their powerful beaks.

When you decide that it's almost time to make your ascent, turn around and swim up over the sandy hill that overlooks the coral ridge. The slope is gentle, and the sand alternates with beautiful coral formations adorned with sponges and gorgonians. But the most outstanding feature is the abundance of remarkable colonies of pillar coral. These corals have a massive structure, but with a soaring, toothed form that resembles a castle with a thousand spires. Their greenish tones stand out clearly against the white sand. It is not uncommon to see large, solitary barracudas in the blue depths behind the coral spires.

The dive ends in this area. You should all gather around the guide,

A

D

D. The angelfish is a sight characteristic of any dive in the Caribbean Sea.

E. These two large, isolated sponges stand on the white sand of the seabed, with a small gorgonian growing at their base.

F. This large coral cluster at about 80 feet (24 meters) deep is surmounted by two large brown sponges.

E

F

who will send up the signal balloon.
Following the line, make your ascent
as the boat hastens to move vertically
above you to signal your position to
the other boats and take you on
board.

A

B

A. This photograph gives some idea of the immensity of this wall, which plunges to inaccessible depths. In the foreground is a splendid tube sponge.

B. You need to swim for a few yards along the plateau before you come to the mooring area at the beginning of the wall.

Hole in the Wall
Roatan

Many believe that Hole in the Wall is one of the real "musts" of Bay Island dives. Whether or not you like this type of dive, one thing is certain: Hole in the Wall is one of the most spectacular parts of the sea. It's more a dive of sensations than an underwater exploration in pursuit of knowledge about the color-ful marine creatures you discover.

This diving area is off the northern coast of Roatan Island, slightly north of beautiful, famous Half Moon Bay. If you examine a nautical map, you'll immediately see that you're in a distinc-tive part of the Honduran coral reef. Here, the reef that borders Roatan Island to the north closely follows the coast, first running northeast-southwest and then turning sharply south. The wall at Hole in the Wall, right at the angle, forms a sort of promontory, a section of reef that juts out and directly overlooks the abyss—and this is what makes this dive so spectacular.

The reef descends gently until it reaches a slope about 50 feet (15 meters) deep. This is more or less the depth you'll find yourself at if you jump in under the boat moored at the buoy. The point you're seeking will be nearby: a deep vertical cleft in the reef that penetrates at least 15 feet

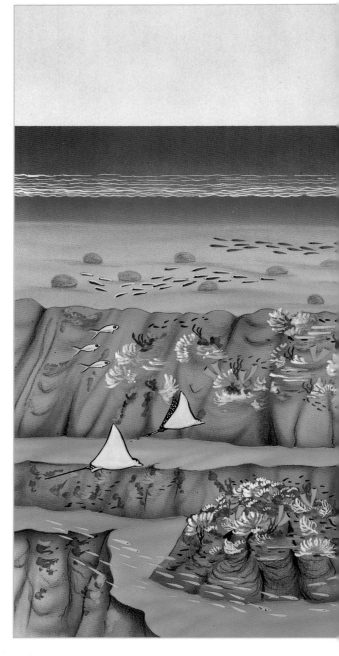

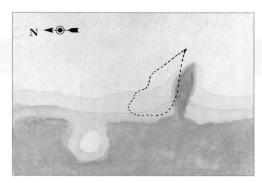

French Harbor

Hole in the Wall
Airport

WEST END POINT

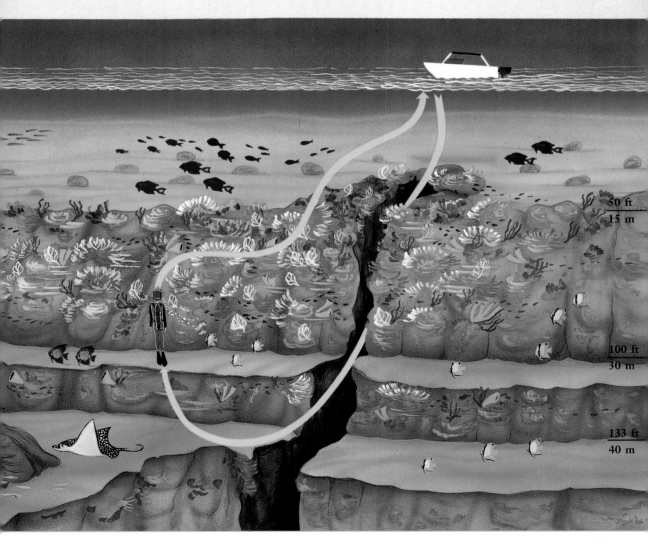

50 ft
15 m

100 ft
30 m

133 ft
40 m

A

B

C

A. A dense school of blue surgeonfish swims over the beautiful corals in the deeper part of the dive.

B. Here is the beginning of the crack that will continue until this beautiful wall reaches great depths.

E

F

(4.5 meters) into the coral structure. Closer to the edge, the crevice is deep but rather narrow. As you descend, the crevice widens and begins to look like a real canyon. It continues to broaden, then tends to narrow a bit on the outside wall, probably due to the growth of corals, which tend to cover the fracture and fuse the two sides.

Descending into the deep blue sea, you'll find yourself in a magically beautiful environment. Everything is still within the canyon. Below you, the sea is a gorgeous deep blue. If you dive here on a day when the water is murky, you will almost certainly see the layer of suspended particles in the first 65 feet (20 meters). As you continue to descend, the water becomes limpid and crystalline, and the murky layer turns into nothing more than a heavy gray cloud over your head that only makes the environment more impressive, illuminated as it is by the diffuse light that filters in from above.

The beauty of the wall's morphology is what makes this descent so fascinating, not the abundance of life, although the canyon also contains beautiful sponges and isolated branches of black coral. As you go deeper, the canyon becomes larger. In some areas, you'll see a steep, sandy floor. Sometimes a flat step makes it seem as if the crevice ends there, on that patch of white sand, but then you'll notice that beyond the step, it once again drops off into the abyss. There is a broad, clear step at about 130 feet (39 meters) deep, and another one just at 200 feet (60 meters). Then a sandy platform ends at 300 feet (90 meters), and after that it drops endlessly into the crystalline water. Of course, your dive will end before that. When you reach about 130 feet (39 meters), you'll

spot a massive coral promontory that protrudes sharply from the crack and the profile of the wall and juts out to the open sea. As you descend, look out to the open sea, and you'll see it on your right. Leave the canyon, but don't forget to stop for a moment and admire the sight of the great fracture in the coral from below.

Head to the isolated coral mass, which has an abundance of life and overlooks the deep sea. From there, continue your dive by swimming to the north, keeping the beautiful wall on your right. Follow it for a while, gradually decreasing the depth, until you reach the edge of the reef. From there, change direction and return to the boat.

D

C. A startled eagle ray flees as divers arrive.

D. This shot highlights both the vastness of the wall and the exceptional transparency of the water.

E. This angelfish is near the drop-off area.

F. A delicate arborescent sponge, photographed in deep water.

A

B

A. The stern of the wreck, in deeper water, lies on its side.

B. An image of the beautiful bow facing Roatan and resting upright on the sea floor.

Wreck of the El Aguila
Roatan

El Aguila is a small vessel that was sunk in the early 1990s, yet another attempt to create an artificial reef that would be a new point of interest for divers. The old mercantile ship was sunk in the water across from Anthony's Key Resort, on the northern coast of the island; it lies on a sandy area just beyond the foot of a beautiful coral wall. Even if you don't enjoy shipwrecks, especially deliberately sunken ships that have no history, you should still explore *El Aguila* for a taste of the impressive power of nature.

Before hurricane Mitch, the wreck was intact and in good condition, a ship resting on a seabed between 105 and 125 feet (32 and 38 meters) deep. Today, the ship is broken in two. The bow is resting upright on the sea floor, the stern tossed to the starboard side, with part of the upper deck pulled out and fallen onto the sand a little farther off. Imagine the violence of waves capable of creating such destruction at a depth of over 100 feet (30 meters), to a ship that was still robust and in excellent condition, with no deterioration or weakening from rust and time.

As usual, a fixed mooring point marks the location of the ship.

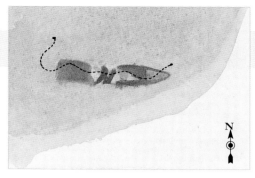

N

FRENCH HARBOR

Wreck of the El Aguila

Airport

WEST END POINT

92 ft
28 m

106 ft
32 m

133 ft
34 m

A

The ship's stern faces the open sea, and the bow faces the reef. Even from the surface you can usually see the dark form of the ship on the sparkling white sand floor. When you complete your descent, you'll find yourself facing the stern's innards, including

B

the quarter-deck and the entry to the engine room. You'll be struck by the fact that almost ten years after the ship was sunk, the wreckage is still clean, with no encrusting or coloniz-ation by sponges, gorgonians, or corals. However, there will almost certainly be two or three large

groupers, not in the least intimidated by divers, who will circle around you curiously. The top of the quarter-deck reaches 92 feet (28 meters), while the seabed is at a depth of 112 feet (34 meters).

If you enjoy exploring shipwrecks, this is for you. Take advantage of the fact that your dive has just begun and your air tank is still almost completely full. Some areas are especially easy to

C

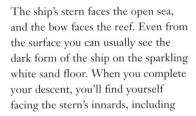

D

enter, and the interior is always spacious and luminous. There isn't much to see inside, except for a few patterns of light that filter in from the portholes and the cracks in the wreckage. If you've gone inside, you'll naturally want to leave through a large opening near the bow, and from there swim toward the other end of the ship. The big groupers will immediately surround you, and you can begin your exploration with them.

There is very little to see in the central part of the wreck, although you should stop occasionally to note the violence the hurricane wrought on the

wreckage, which is incredibly con-torted, yet still solid and in excellent condition. Unlike the stern, the bow is quite spectacular. Lying intact on the white sand, it is especially impressive if you descend to the sandy floor, between 100 and 105 feet (30 and 32 meters) deep, and stop for a minute to admire it from the bottom. Move along the sand to right under the cutwater. You won't be able to

E

A. At the stern, the diver can admire the great hoists that were used to load and unload cargo.

B. A diver explores the windows of the bridge in the stern section.

C. The skylights in the engine room can be easily identified.

D. Inside the engine room of the little merchant ship. Entry is quick and easy.

E. From the bow of the old ship, take a look at the surround-ing seabed.

F. A red sponge uses the ship's wreckage as a base for develop-ment. Not much benthic life has colonized the ship.

miss a great coral mass with a large green moray living beneath it.

When you reach this point, you have two possibilities. You can either proceed in the same direction and finish your dive by retracing your path up the reef wall, or you can return to the deck of the bow and swim to the stern, staying at a depth of about 82 feet (25 meters) to admire the wreck in its entirety.

FRENCH HARBOR

Diving with the Dolphins
(Anthony's Key Resort)

Airport

WEST END POINT

Anthony's Key Resort

A. A large dolphin has just passed through the middle of the group of divers. **A**

B. Here are the large, closed bodies of water where the dolphins live in semi-captivity. **B**

50 ft

15 m

Diving with the Dolphins
Roatan

Very few animals in Neptune's realm are as fascinating to humans as dolphins. Perhaps it's their incredible elegance, their air of perennial cheerfulness and playfulness, the fact that unlike many other creatures, they can "talk." Perhaps it's simply because they are so clearly mammals.

This dive near Roatan Island has justly become world-famous, because here it is possible to meet these fascinating creatures in their natural environment. On the northern coast of Roatan is Anthony's Key Resort, which is not just a resort but also a large dolphin study and training center that even has a small museum. Anyone can interact with dolphins here, in shallow or deep water, by snorkeling or scuba diving. Naturally, we have focused on scuba diving here.

The experience begins with a long briefing as the divers sit with their legs dangling in the water. In this way you can familiarize yourself with the dolphins, who will approach, allow

A. After a few moments, the dolphins approach fearlessly and even allow themselves to be petted.

B. There is no need to move. In fact, it may be better to remain motionless on the floor and wait for the dolphins to approach.

C. The dolphins seem to enjoy themselves with the divers, racing back and forth past them.

A

B

C

themselves to be petted, and do some exercises, guided by the trainer.

It's important to clarify a number of things before entering the water. Never exhibit aggressive behavior, and always stay still and calm in one position, allowing the dolphins to approach at their own pace. During the briefing, you'll be given some

interesting information on the biology of these creatures and their behavior. Soon you'll be ready to take off in the boat, heading out to the open sea, and you'll equip yourself quickly.

The boat stops at a point where there is a vast sandy area about 50 feet (15 meters) deep. Jump into the crystalline water as the dolphins begin to gather around the boat. They swim in pairs, keeping a slight distance. You should try to reach the bottom quickly, so you don't distract them from the rest of the group. Kneel on the bottom, and you'll see them coming at full speed, beginning to circle all around you. They pass again and again, slipping right into the group of divers and allowing themselves to be stroked.

As you photograph the dolphins, you may wonder if they really appreciate your interest and enjoy being petted. After all, they aren't house cats. Perhaps we'll never know the answer, but the fact remains that the dolphins at least don't appear to be disturbed by the attention from

divers. Still, their bodies bear marks and scratches that seem to call for extra care in touching them. The dive lasts twenty minutes. Then the trainer returns to his small boat, followed by the dolphins. The divers remain on the sea floor and watch them disappear in the wake of the little motorboat.

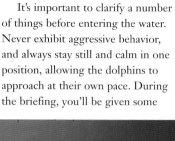

D. Here are the dolphins in the water, quite close to the divers as they swim over a luminous, white sand seabed.

E. The two dolphins swim closely around the divers, playing together.

F. Here, a curious individual comes to look at its reflection in the camera's lens.

Peter's Place and Bear's Den FRENCH HARBOR

Airport

WEST END POINT

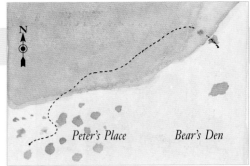

Peter's Place Bear's Den

A. Small groupers can be found all over Peter's Place at very shallow depths.

B. Gorgonians grow at depths of over 65 feet (20 meters), where the broad plateau begins to drop into the wall.

A

B

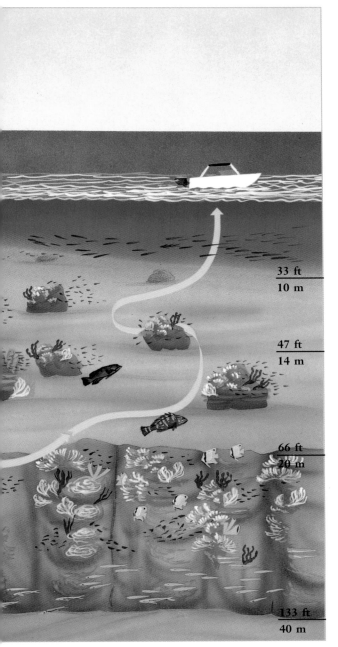

33 ft
10 m

47 ft
14 m

66 ft
20 m

133 ft
40 m

Peter's Place and Bear's Den
Roatan

Here we are again on the northern coast of Roatan, ready for two more beautiful dives on the seabeds directly east of Front Porch, which is famous for its dives with the dolphins of Anthony's Key Resort.

The point farther west is Peter's Place. Here, the seabed turns to coral after the interruption of Front Porch Reef. The broad, sandy sea floor begins to sprout a myriad of stony coral formations, which rest on the sediment that extends for a few hundred yards toward the open sea before encountering a slope 65 feet (20 meters) deep that rapidly drops to 115 to 130 feet (35 to 39 meters). Peter's Place is famous for its groupers, which are usually quite friendly and easily approached. You will also see schools of jacks and a large number of gigantic, solitary porgies. Probably all these fish are attracted by the fact that feed for dolphins is thrown into the sea not far from here.

The distinctive feature of Bear's Den is a typical passageway into the reef, which is quite fragmented and jagged here, leading you right to the middle of the wall. Let's take a brief look at the itinerary you should follow and what you can expect to see on the sea floor. Current permitting, we

A. *A bold block of pillar coral characteristic of this coral plateau.*

B. *A school of jacks swims freely in the open water.*

C. *There are larger groupers at Peter's as well, but they are a little more suspicious than the smaller ones.*

D. *These cracks distinguish Bear's Den and lead to the middle of the wall.*

A

B

and the reef rises to 3 feet (1 meter) from the surface. As soon as you jump into the water, you'll find yourself above an extremely varied sea floor with an irregular, quite spectacular display of coral pinnacles rising up from trenches in the sandy seabed. Depths vary from 6 or 10 feet (2 or 3 meters) to 35 feet (11 meters) in the deeper areas. Your guide will show you an open trench in the limestone that you can explore. Toward the coast, you will see bare limestone rock, probably carved and smoothed by the waves. Several feet toward the open sea, if you look closely within this deep, narrow depression, you'll see a hole in the limestone, which becomes increasingly distinct as you approach. You'll soon see that it's more

suggest beginning your dive at Bear's Den and then swimming to Peter's Place, where the boat can pick you up. You can still start from the other side if you want, since there are usually no strong currents in these areas.

A completely flat, circular limestone rock tells you where to start your dive. The buoy at Bear's Den is just a few yards east of the rock. The sea floor in this area is quite shallow,

C

D

E. *A curious Nassau grouper hovers motionless, watching a diver.*

F. *At very shallow depths, a small gorgonian in a close-up taken with a wide-angle lens looks gigantic.*

than just a hole, but a narrow fracture in the rock over 35 feet (11 meters) long that leads right to the middle of the wall. Inside the crack, the rocks are smooth and polished. You won't need a flashlight to light the way, as there are not many animals to discover. This place owes its beauty to the patterns of light filtering in from the exit; the entrance is under a vault and squeezed between two steep cliffs, and is thus rather dark.

Go single file through the narrow passage, and you'll come out more or less at the middle of a wall that plunges 80 to 100 feet (25 to 30 meters) onto a gently sloping floor. The exit is

between 46 and 53 feet (14 and 16 meters) deep. From here, start swimming with the wall to your left. During the first stretch, try not to descend too deep, as above a depth of 50 feet (15 meters) are numerous cracks in the coral that are quite spectacular, especially in the morning.

Continuing southwest, you'll see that the slope gradually descends from about 30 to 65 feet (9 to 20 meters) deep, and the plateau area becomes much broader. Leave the wall and swim over the plateau, which has a wealth of stony coral formations and fish and is brightly illuminated by the light reflected on the sandy sea floor.

You have now reached what is considered another diving area: Peter's Place. If you're lucky and the day is right, you could meet a multitude of friendly groupers, who are not intimidated by divers in the slightest and will swim all around you.

F

Wreck of the Prince Albert
Roatan

L
ike all the most well-known
wrecks in the Bay Islands, the
Prince Albert, a small merchant
ship, was sunk intentionally to provide
a new habitat for many species and an
additional point of interest for scuba
divers. The little *Prince Albert*, about
200 feet (60 meters) long, was sunk in
1987 not far off the southern coast of
Roatan Island, right across from the
Coco View Resort. It is located in a
channel with a sandy floor, protected
on one side by the coral reef that
extends for several hundred yards
beyond the shoreline, and by Fantasy
Island on the other side.

A very shallow area was purposely
chosen to sink the small merchant ship;
it lies on a sea floor that runs from a
maximum of 60 feet (18 meters) to a
minimum of 46 feet (14 meters) in
depth, while the upper deck structures
rise to 40 feet (12 meters) in the stern
area and 25 feet (8 meters) in the bow.
Diving directly onto the wreck is
usually not recommended. Instead,
enter the water where the reef drop-
off creates a sharp angle between the
south- and west-facing walls, then
reenters toward the coast.

Here the reef is truly shallow, at
times rising just a couple of inches
from the surface. Contrary to what

FRENCH HARBOR

Wreck of the Prince Albert

▼

FANTASY ISLAND

Airport

WEST END POINT

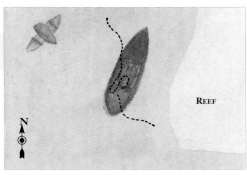

REEF

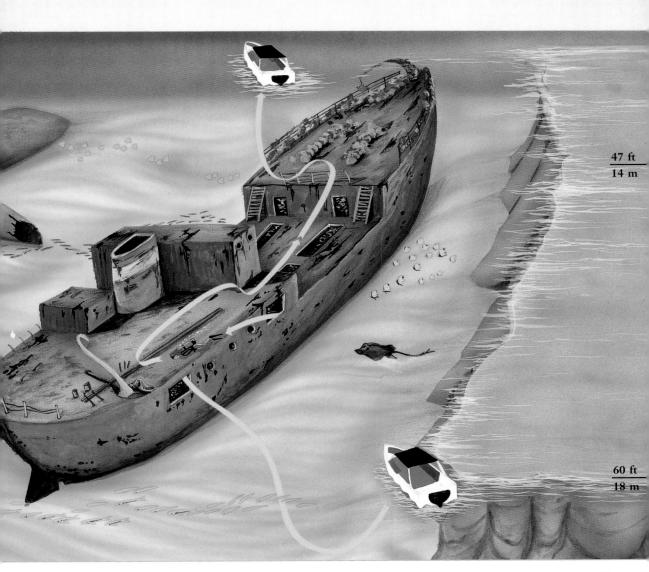

47 ft
———
14 m

60 ft
———
18 m

one might expect, the wall is quite beautiful, with the alternating cliffs and promontories creating a spectacular morphology, and teeming with life. Everything depends on visibility here, which can be excellent or quite mediocre and may change in a matter of minutes. Swim with the wall to your right anywhere between 50 and 100 feet (15 to 30 meters) deep. It's an extremely easy swim that takes you right on top of the wreck's stern, lying in the deepest area. The little ship rests in a sailing position and is perfectly vertical.

The stern is certainly the most interesting part to visit, as the deck is almost entirely unencrusted and lifeless. By contrast, the stern is literally covered in a complex mixture of gorgonians and sponges. As soon as you arrive, you're sure to notice the

guardrail and a pair of richly encrusted capstans, while on the starboard side you can visit a medium-size green moray that has found a comfortable home in the arm of a tack bumpkin. A large grouper at least two and a half feet (80 centimeters) long resides in

A. Here we are at the bow of this fine wreck, resting upright on the sea floor.

B. Another image of the stern of the Prince Albert.

C. The airplane sunk in the vicinity. Quite frankly, it is not an interesting wreck.

D. The bow of the Prince Albert looks like a luxuriant, somewhat disorderly and unkempt garden.

E. Tube-shaped blue sponges grow on the stern of the ship.

the narrow port-side corridor, easy to see but impossible to approach.

When you're tired of wandering around the upper deck, you can go down along the side and enter the ship. Inside, you can explore three different levels, but the most beautiful sights are the patterns of light from the port holes and the whirling of a dense school of silversides. From the stern, swim along the deck. It really isn't worth entering the ship through the long openings there, but the gorgonians clustered around the capstans of the bow itself are quite nice. This area is only 26 feet (8 meters) deep. A rope runs from the bulwark in the forward

area on the port side. If you follow it, you'll find the remains of an airplane. This is another artificial structure that was deliberately sunk, but unfortunately it offers very little interest.

On the starboard side of the ship, you'll notice some rhomboidal structures, which were especially designed to provide practice in buoyancy control. The trick is to go through the rhomboids in particular positions, then remain motionless inside each one. Looking at them is a reminder that pinpoint buoyancy control is the first skill to master for any diver who wants to avoid destroying the reef.

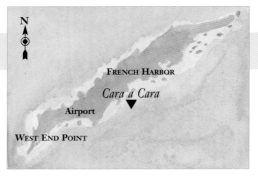

French Harbor

Cara a Cara

Airport

West End Point

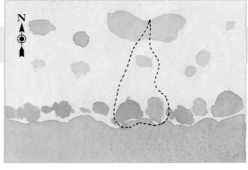

A. A large shark approaches the divers, attracted by the bait. Note the richness of the coral seabed. **A**

B. With their backs protected by a rise, the divers wait for the sharks. They are armed with plastic bats in case the fish become too aggressive. **B**

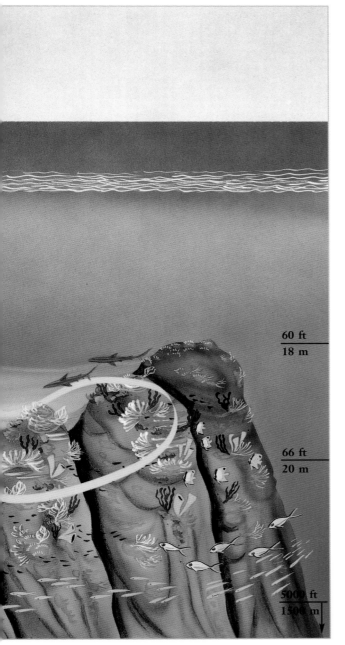

Cara a Cara
Roatan

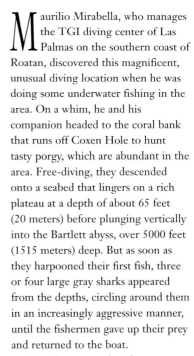

60 ft
18 m

66 ft
20 m

5000 ft
1500 m

Maurilio Mirabella, who manages the TGI diving center of Las Palmas on the southern coast of Roatan, discovered this magnificent, unusual diving location when he was doing some underwater fishing in the area. On a whim, he and his companion headed to the coral bank that runs off Coxen Hole to hunt tasty porgy, which are abundant in the area. Free-diving, they descended onto a seabed that lingers on a rich plateau at a depth of about 65 feet (20 meters) before plunging vertically into the Bartlett abyss, over 5000 feet (1515 meters) deep. But as soon as they harpooned their first fish, three or four large gray sharks appeared from the depths, circling around them in an increasingly aggressive manner, until the fishermen gave up their prey and returned to the boat.

Maurilio returned to the area the next day, with air tanks and no harpoon. The sharks were there, wandering around stony corals and gorgonians, but never came too close. So Maurilio began bringing them fish, and the sharks became increasingly confident. Depending on the season and time, various sharks showed up: sometimes menacing bull sharks, sometimes small whitetip sharks, and always five gray sharks. These were quite beautiful and large, from 6.5 feet (2 meters) to the 10-foot (3 meter)-long male, which Maurilio named Ugo.

Having become a habitual visitor to the area, Maurilio found an ideal point to lead visitors to the five gray sharks that always showed up. They can now recognize the noise of the boat and are already waiting on the seabed for divers to arrive. Just look toward the bottom right after you jump into the water, and you'll spot their shapes from the surface.

This is not a dive for large groups, so dive in groups of three or four, and no more than eight. Everyone is given a three-foot long PVC stick for personal protection if the sharks become too aggressive, although so far this hasn't happened. Descend together along the mooring line until you come to a seabed exactly 65 feet (20 meters) deep. Line up on the floor with your back facing a little wall 10 feet (3 meters) high and about 100 feet (30 meters) long, which will prevent a shark from unexpectedly coming up behind you.

You'll have watched the sharks during your entire descent, swimming peacefully along the seabed and distancing themselves more and more as you approach. Once you reach the seabed, you can just barely glimpse their shapes in the distance. Taking advantage of this, the guide will position the divers along the ridge and place the fish on the sea floor, protected by the rocks, so it is not too easy for

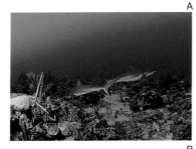

A

B

C

D

A. Two sharks approach together, but the presence of the photographer intimidates them, and they veer off before they reach the bait.

B. After grabbing the morsel, the shark quickly veers off to a distance before making a second approach.

C. A shark moves elegantly and swiftly among the gorgonians.

D. Two sharks in the distance in the water of Cara a Cara.

the sharks to grab it in a single bite and vanish in an instant.

It seems that these elegant, menacing sea creatures understand when everything is ready and they can finally approach. As soon as the guide takes his place with the others, you'll see the first shark slip in very close to the group of divers. It will be followed by a second and then a third . . . . From your position, you'll be able to mark the dead fish by the cloud of small fish that aggressively and frenetically feast for a few minutes before being forced to disappear and take shelter from the first

E   F

lightning attack of the sharks.

And this is where the show begins. One by one, these sea predators fall upon the morsels brought for them. They calmly gather up the bones and swallow them voraciously. They circle in close rings, come very close to the divers, but show no aggressiveness or any signs of nervousness. Evidently the facts that the fish are dead and that there is an abundance of food for all prevents the feeding frenzy that sometimes makes the fascinating spectacle of shark feeding dangerous.

When they finish the fish on the sea floor, the sharks linger, continuing

to swim slowly and elegantly around the group of divers. Usually a dive lasts about twenty minutes, which approaches the computers' no-decompression limit, and the sharks return to the blue depths, full and satisfied.

E. An angelfish moves serenely along the seabed, heedless of sea predators.

F. Here is the drop-off that begins the splendid wall. The wealth of little fish is exceptionally surprising.

FRENCH HARBOR

Mary's Place

▼

Airport

WEST END POINT

N

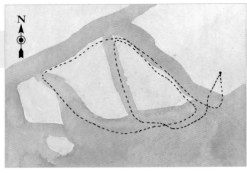

N

26 ft
8 m

40 ft
12 m

50 ft
15 m

85 ft
26 m

116 ft
35 m

A. One of the cracks among the corals so characteristic of Mary's Place.

B. This beautiful sea anemone can be found at the exit of the second canyon, just a few feet deep.

A

B

Mary's Place
Roatan

Mary's Place, definitely the dive that symbolizes Roatan, runs along a spectacular wall teeming with life, in water swarming with fish. It's off the southern coast of the island, an area where mangrove forests rise beyond the rocks, forming a series of channels that will shelter you from the wind and waves as you head northeast to your diving area.

As usual, a buoy signals where you should enter the water. The buoy is attached to a coral floor 26 feet (8 meters) deep that you can clearly see from the boat as you gaze into the crystalline water. Make your descent and head east rather than to the drop-off you'll see to the south, marked by the intense blue color of the sea. After several feet, you'll find yourself suspended over a wall more than 100 feet (30 meters) deep on a broad, sandy slide.

Along this spectacular wall you'll find enormous, beautiful gorgonian fans, arborescent red and brown sponges that grow knotted together, great barrel sponges, and spectacular violet-colored vase sponges that rise up from the middle of the wall. Around you, an uncommonly large number of fish swim by—yellow jacks, large barracudas, and dense groups of

your right. After several feet you'll find yourself facing a narrow crevice in the corals. This crevice runs from the top of the reef at about 35 feet (10 meters) deep to the bottom at 100 feet (30 meters). It is narrow, tight, and jagged, and broken into recesses and protrusions. Branches of black coral and sponges stand out everywhere from the wall.

A. A coral prospers within a large barrel sponge.

B. Sponges and gorgonians of this type grow abundantly right at the exit of the cracks, where they can find particles of food carried by the current that flows among the rocks.

C. A close-up of a threatening-looking but harmless barracuda.

D. A Nassau grouper on the coral plateau swims together with a diver.

E. This is the exit to one of the canyons, where a myriad of little silver fish gather. For many years, this diving area was closed to allow the coral to recover from the damage it had suffered.

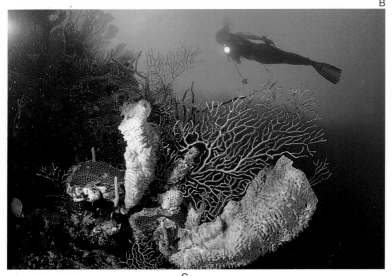

little blue parrotfish. Not only that, there are brown groupers, Nassau groupers, dogtooth groupers, and large red porgies. You won't be able to restrain your surprise and enthusiasm.

As you halt your descent between 65 and 100 feet (20 to 30 meters) deep, continue swimming with the wall on

At the entrance to the fracture, large gorgonian fans open like curtains. Move inside very cautiously, and be extremely careful not to bump the walls or swim near the floor, which will raise a cloud of sediment. In short, try not to do anything to ruin this splendid underwater environment. Remember that this diving area was closed to divers for five whole years, after years of diving had damaged the ecosystem.

With extreme caution, follow the over 165 spectacular feet (50 meters) of the canyon until you reach a sandy saddle 85 feet (26 meters) deep, from

which you can look out over the steep wall on the southern side of the reef. Now head left, maintaining your depth, until you encounter a second crevice that once again breaks the coral promontory in two. Turn sharply right, go inside, and follow the crevice, which is narrower and shorter than the first one, but perhaps a little more colorful and full of life, until you once again exit on the wall facing east. You are now on the sandy slope you saw in the beginning. Keeping the wall to your left, move along a several dozen feet until you find yourself back at the entry to the first crack.

For some reason, when you arrive from this direction, the opening in the coral seems even more beautiful and filled with sponges and gorgonians. Stop for a minute in this lovely place and take a few photos, then enter the beautiful crevice again. Swim carefully now, because you don't want to go all the way to the end, where the sandy rise 85 feet (26 meters) deep leads you to the outer wall.

Just before this, turn abruptly to your left, making an almost 180-degree turn. You'll find another small canyon that you certainly didn't notice the first time; enter it now.

This is the shortest and narrowest crevice, but there's a surprise inside: right at the end, close to where the crack exits to the open sea, there is a spectacular school of thousands of silversides swarming together as if they were a single organism, glittering as the sunlight filters down on them from above. Continue, and the fish will let you pass through, accompanying you almost to the aperture that leads right into the eastern wall. From here, swim over the sandy slide, keeping the wall to the left, and retrace your steps back to the mooring buoy on the plateau.

FRENCH HARBOR

Airport

Pablo's Place

WEST END POINT

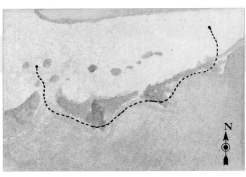

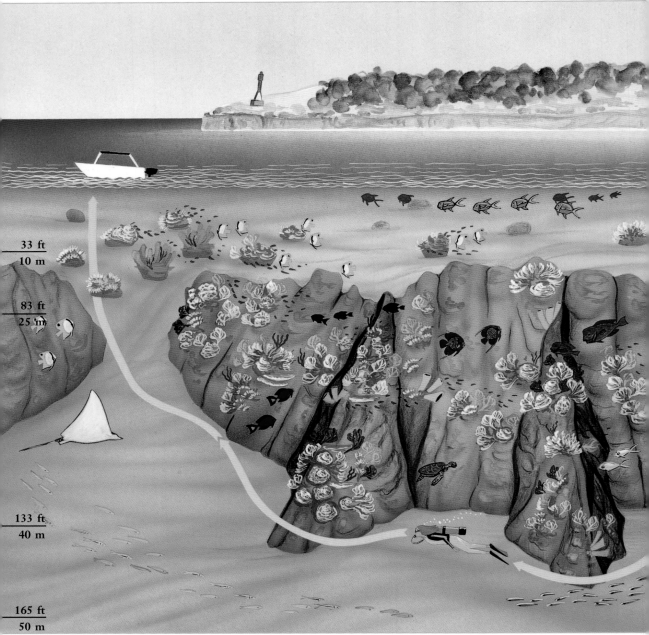

33 ft
10 m

83 ft
25 m

133 ft
40 m

165 ft
50 m

A. There are beautiful, rich coral formations on the plateau as you swim toward West End.

B. A large gorgonian protrudes from a rocky promontory.

A

B

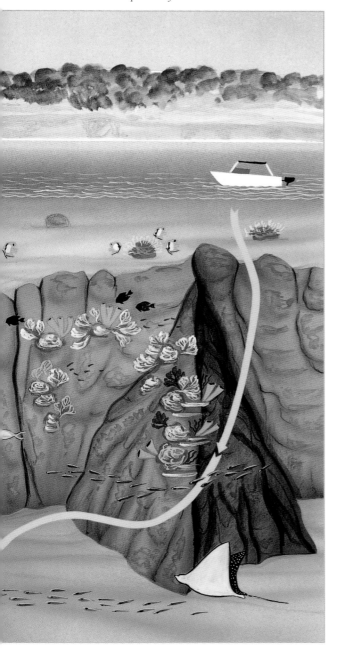

Pablo's Place
Roatan

The dive described below takes place at the extreme southwestern tip of Roatan Island, an especially interesting area due to the presence of moderate currents that carry in a certain abundance of pelagic fish.

The dive begins at about a quarter of a mile from the tip of West End. Because of the current, drift dives are more common here; let yourself be carried by the current, and the boat will follow your bubbles and promptly pick you up after the dive is over.

As usual at Roatan, the water is quite clear, and you can easily see the floor about 50 feet (15 meters) below. The seabed descends gently, richly covered with gorgonians swarming with coral fish, most commonly blue and red parrotfish, angelfish, and butterflyfish. The slope clearly changes into a wall at a depth of 50 to 76 feet (15 to 23 meters). Drop to a depth of 83 feet to 100 feet (25 to 30 meters) and begin your exploration. You'll immediately note that below you, the drop-off ends at a depth of between 132 and 165 feet (40 to 50 meters), on a sandy, sloping sea floor of little interest. But the coral buttresses of the wall are most impressive as they extend from the general outline of the drop-off and reach out to the open

A

B

C

E

D

sea, creating a series of ridges squeezed between the two promontories.

Of course, the most interesting areas to explore are the ones that extend out to sea, beyond the profile of the wall, where benthic life is the most amazing. You'll find large gorgonian fans and sponges of every type, and small, brilliant yellow gorgonians that live at the base of their larger cousins. In the depressions of the wall, especially the shallow areas closest to the drop-off, you'll find a great abundance of sea plumes and large barrel sponges that have colonized sandy ledges on the wall. Among the corals, you can often spot large sponges, green and hawksbill turtles, angelfish, and yellow snappers. Fish are more abundant in the depressions of the wall than in the protrusions.

The current continues to carry you southwest, where you can find dense schools of yellowtail snappers, barracudas, eagle rays, and turtles. You'll also note that as you gradually approach the tip, the sea floor changes radically. The vertical wall begins to look fragmented, and the interior areas transform into gently sloping valleys with sandy floors. Take the opportunity to decrease your depth and stop at around 50 feet (15 meters), turning your attention to the sandy floor, where you'll see a profusion of isolated corals and sea plumes. Then shift your gaze to the coral promontories, which are now much more accentuated and defined. You'll see many more stony corals on the promontories now, including lettuce coral, brain coral, and in particular the lovely pillar coral that is so characteristic of these waters. Among the corals, you'll discover many reef fish, which become much more numerous as you near the point. You can also spot solitary barracuda in the limpid water as they float motionless over patches of white sand, while schools of jacks and turtles may appear out of the blue depths at any moment to pay you a visit.

Stay near the rest of the group and the guide will send a balloon up to the waiting boat, which will allow it to identify your diving group while you make your safety stop.

F

G

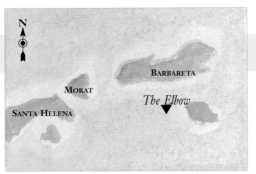

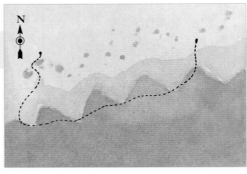

A. An aerial view of Barbareta and the reefs surrounding it.

B. A soft gorgonian branch grows between large barrel sponges. A

B

The Elbow
Barbareta

Barbareta is a tiny island that has a beach resort, but is otherwise uninhabited. It rises from the sea not far from the northeast tip of Roatan, almost as if it were an appendage, connected by a complex system of reefs. It's definitely worthwhile to organize a few dives at Barbareta when you come to Roatan on a cruise, as the island and its lagoons and seabeds are quite beautiful. These features make for a more than pleasant excursion even if you don't dive. The reef around the island is quite extensive and extends far out into the open sea, offering divers many excellent opportunities. The dive described here is just a sample of what these lovely sea floors have to offer.

Start on the southern side of Barbareta, outside the lagoon, beyond the reef that connects the platform to the wall with a drop-off at about 35 feet (11 meters) deep. The Elbow is near the eastern tip, beyond the islands known as Pigeon Cays. If you come here by boat on a fine day when the sun is shining and the sea is calm, you'll find a marvelous sight: a white sand floor about 35 feet (11 meters) deep reflecting back up to the surface in a wondrous manner, giving the

crystalline water a brilliant emerald color. Enter the water over the sandy seabed decorated with large stony corals and luxuriant *Pseudopterogorgia* sea feathers, which look like palms in a desert oasis. Sometimes large silvery snappers hover motionless, almost as if they're enjoying the shade of the sea plumes. Right on the plateau, you'll often find an uncommonly gigantic, very friendly hawksbill turtle, a permanent resident here.

promontories and recesses. At about 35 feet (11 meters) the seabed drops to 50 feet (15 meters) in a steep vertical plunge, then continues down to a floor almost 130 feet (39 meters) deep, in a gentle, very undulating slope. Descend to the desired depth. Before deciding what direction to take, check to see if there is a current, and adjust your movements accordingly; strong currents are not at all uncommon in this area.

The coral bank is quite rich. You'll find the usual profusion of colorful sponges alternating with beautiful gorgonian branches, as well as enormous, isolated barrel sponges. The Elbow at Barbareta is the ideal place to find a myriad of fish. Jacks and Bermuda chub from the Caranx

A

F

C

B

D

A. In this image of deep seabeds, an orange sponge shines in the camera flash.

B. Another image of this extraordinary environment, set off by the clear water.

C. A colony of annelids grows at the base of this gorgonian.

D. A beautiful brain coral grows on a shallow seabed illuminated by the reflection of the sunlight on the light sand.

E. In deep water, a large mass is covered with arborescent sponges.

F. Admiring the tongues of sand among the coral ridges, we make our descent.

G. You don't need a deep descent for sights like this, which reveal the richness of the waters off the Bay Islands.

As you swim toward the edge, you'll immediately see that it does not follow a straight, regular profile but is very jagged, with a number of

and Kyphosus genus respectively are especially common in this area. There is also an abundance of snappers and greater amberjack.

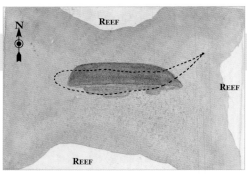

A. This moray is the resident homeowner. Don't be frightened by its appearance, as it is actually quite harmless and friendly.

B. Dense schools of silver fish live within the Jado Trader.

A

B

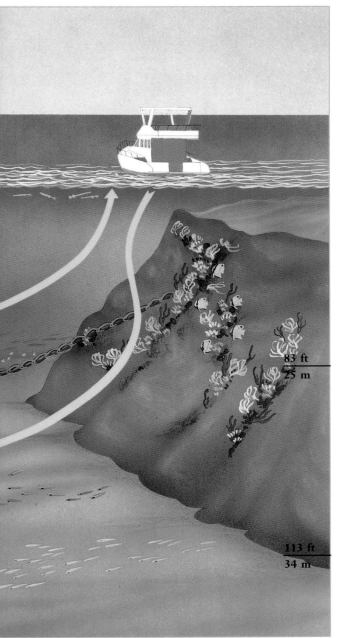

83 ft
25 m

113 ft
34 m

Wreck of the Jado Trader
Guanaja

The story of the *Jado Trader*, a small mercantile ship that sank south of the port of Guanaja, includes a bit of adventure and mystery. The *Jado Trader*, a small fruit transporter, sailed among the islands and various ports of Central America, until the authorities stopped the ship, found a load of drugs, and discovered that the ship had been trafficking drugs for who knows how long under its cover of transporting tropical fruit. The *Jado Trader* was then confiscated and remained neglected at the end of the port for years.

In the mid-1980s, some local operators bought the ship and sunk it to create an artificial reef. The *Jado Trader* was towed to its final destination, a broad, sandy area surrounded by three spectacular coral pinnacles that rise from the seabed from about 112 feet (34 meters) to an average of 50 feet (15 meters) deep. The ship lies on its starboard side, the port side rising toward the surface to a depth of about 82 feet (25 meters), its bow lying on the sea floor several feet from the base of a coral peak that rises vertically from there to 46 feet (14 meters).

The top of the reef is clearly visible across the transparent water,

A

B

A. The bow of the Jado Trader *as it appears after a descent along the mooring line.*

B. *Like docile puppies, large groupers* accompany divers *during their descent and ascent.*

C. *A view of the ship at the stern, below the now horizontal masts.*

D. *An image of the colorful stern capstans. The upper structures of the* Jado Trader *are in fact now completely covered with benthic organisms.*

E. *A moray has made its home among the structures of the wreck.*

while the sandy bottom still seems somewhat obscured. Go down several feet and look west. You'll immediately see the form of the ship, with its bow facing you and looking spectacular in the azure water, with the upper portion covered with sea plumes. Move west toward the stern. During the entire descent, two or three large groupers,

who are quite accustomed to divers and will sometimes even eat from your hand, accompany you to the ship.

Spend a short time at the bow to take a look at the capstans, which are thickly encrusted and now populated by a large number of coral fish. Right over the upper capstan on the port side, there is a cleaning station where

parrotfish and small groupers stop. Head to the smokestack area, now near the stern, which is by far the most interesting area. One of the features of this wreck is a hold completely full of silversides. A dense school moves in a truly spectacular manner in the beam of your lamp, which is great for photographers.

Continue your exploration, and you'll discover the stern area, with dense colonies of sponges and other invertebrates. There is an abundance of large blue parrotfish and angelfish. Inside, you can still distinguish the remains of a gas stove overturned on the floor and a bath that now looks bizarre, hanging as it is on what is now the ceiling of the overturned ship. You've now used up half of your diving time at depths between 100 and 112 feet (30 to 34 meters), and so it's time to head to your surfacing point.

C

D

Be careful when you approach the ship structures or enter them; two gigantic green morays live here, and won't hesitate to give you what appears to be a menacing greeting. But don't be intimidated; they are simply used to seeing scuba divers and taking food from their hands, and actually have no hostile intentions.

Go past the stern and stop for a minute to admire the propeller and rudder and observe the great chain that trails onto a distant reef from the stern, then ascend up the port side. You are now at 82 feet (25 meters) and can swim slowly to the bow, admiring the life that flourishes in the forest of gorgonians that have completely covered the upper part of the ship. Soon you'll see the shape of the reef. Head toward it, and you'll easily find the ascent line.

E

MANGROVE BIGHT

SAVANNA BIGHT

Jim's Silver Lode ▼

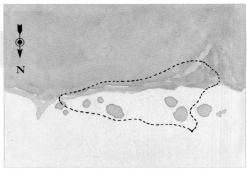

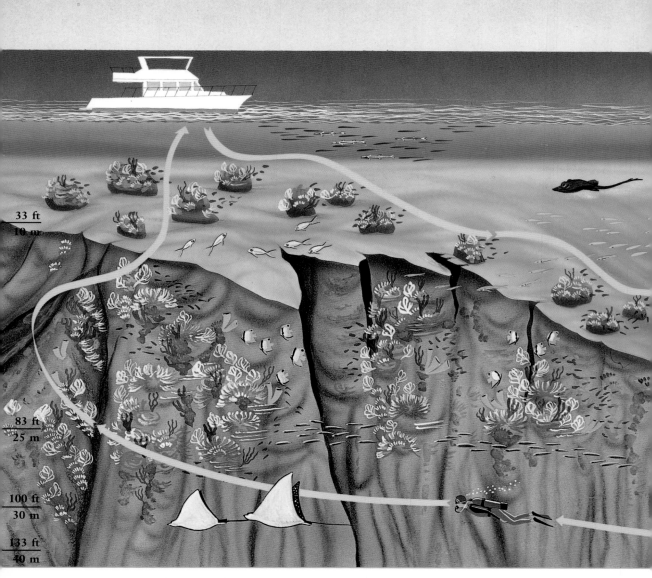

33 ft
10 m

83 ft
25 m

100 ft
30 m

133 ft
40 m

A. You'll find yourself on the lush coral plateau as soon as you enter the water. Here are huge gorgonian sea fans.

B. A large sponge protrudes from the imposing vertical wall.

A

B

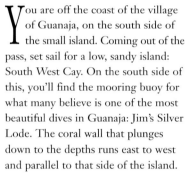

Jim's Silver Lode
Guanaja

You are off the coast of the village of Guanaja, on the south side of the small island. Coming out of the pass, set sail for a low, sandy island: South West Cay. On the south side of this, you'll find the mooring buoy for what many believe is one of the most beautiful dives in Guanaja: Jim's Silver Lode. The coral wall that plunges down to the depths runs east to west and parallel to that side of the island.

The buoy is anchored onto a seabed of luxuriant coral shoals alternating with patches of sand at about 30 feet (9 meters) deep. Descend along the mooring line and swim east. The seabed is quite uneven and spectacular, full of rocky crests covered with gorgonians and populated by coral fish, alternating with valleys with white sand floors. Going east, you'll see that the average depth increases very gradually. Slowly the sandy base exceeds 50 feet (15 meters). Keep your eyes peeled throughout your exploration, as stingrays are especially common here, and you may see them motionless on the sea floor, covered in sand. You need to look closely to spot them, but they are almost always here.

Continue your exploration under the watchful eyes of a few small, solitary barracuda. Proceed east until

B

you find yourself before a large sandy valley that plunges steadily toward the south. Change direction and head south, descending along the sandy floor and keeping the shoals to the right, and head toward a line of stony coral structures that you'll see before you. If you stay close to the seabed, you should come to one of the crevices that open in the coral. This is the most spectacular part of your dive. Beyond the crevice, you'll see nothing but the deep blue sea, with the floor seeming to vanish beyond the rocks.

As soon as you leave the crevice, you'll come to the breathtakingly

A

E

gorgeous wall, which is quite vertical here. You will be at a depth of about 82 feet (25 meters). Below you, the wall meets the sandy floor, which continues to drop steeply to depths of 165 feet (50 meters), after passing several feet of overhang that creates an elongated cavern at the base of the wall. To your right, toward the west, the wall climbs up to well over your head.

C

A. An angelfish on the upper plateau is followed by a diver.

B. We have often encountered eagle rays at the end of this dive.

D

In the afternoon, you'll be treated to a spectacular sight at this point, with the wall in the shadows and the sun lying low over the upper part of the slope, looking like a brilliant silver disk. It illuminates the gorgonians against the light, emphasizing their forms and cutting them off from the black base of the wall. Swim west at a depth of about 100 feet (30 meters), admiring the large organ pipe sponges and colorful gorgonian fans and enjoying this beautiful wall with its marvelously impressive form.

As you swim, always watch what's happening in the blue depths, as this is an ideal place to see large eagle rays. Spice up your dive by making a multi-level exploration, decreasing your depth as you proceed westward. After a hundred feet or so, when you'll have risen to a depth of about 65 feet (20 meters), you'll see that the wall begins to look less unified and more frag-mented, leaving space for the formation of rocky spurs extending into the open sea. While not overly large, they are teeming with life. As you further decrease your depth, you'll find yourself on the gorgeous plateau, where you can admire large gorgonians and spectacular pillar corals. If you've done things right, you should now find yourself right under your boat.

C. As you make your ascent, you're sure to see numerous, extensive coral formations covering the wall.

D. A beautiful colored sponge has grown on a coral.

E. Rays are common in the sandy areas that lead to the wall.

THE SEA LIFE OF
BELIZE AND HONDURAS

A right angle formed by the coast of Central America delimits one of the most fascinating areas of the Caribbean Sea. This underwater paradise is created by the Honduran coastline, where the coral reefs are unusually large for this tropical region of the Atlantic.

At the extreme south, almost as if following boundaries imposed by man, the reef stops, but not the underwater wonders. In Honduras, all you have to do is move farther out to sea, away from the influence of fresh water that flows out from the coastal rivers, limiting coral development, and go to the Bay Islands of Honduras. These islands, Roatan, Guanaja, and Utila, are suspended over water hundreds of yards deep, where coral communities form a backdrop for the passage of an abundance of pelagic fauna, primarily mantas, tunas, sharks, barracudas, and the ever-present jacks through the pristine waters.

Belize was one of the first countries to introduce ecotourism and environmental protection programs, creating over twenty protected areas that in many cases offer an extraordinary synthesis of this country's natural environments, all arising from a conjunction of land and sea. Purely for

reasons of convenience, they can be divided into four separate habitats: the coast, the internal lagoons, the coral reefs, and the atolls.

The actual coast consists of lagoons fringed by rings of sand, estuaries, and river deltas bordered by rich vegetation that eventually becomes the forests of Belize, inhabited by jaguars, tapirs, pumas, toucans, monkeys, and an infinite variety of birds. The lagoons that lie north and south of Belize City form transition zones for coral habitats. The shallower areas are dominated by vast meadows of underwater plants (*Thalassia testudinum, Syringodium filiforme, Halodule* sp.) that prove irresistible to many herbivorous fish and mollusks like the large *Strombus gigas* (known throughout the Caribbean as queen conch); turtles, which are still quite common on the region's beaches; and especially the rare manatees, who find these lagoons and neighboring mangrove forests, with four different species of mangroves, to be an ideal habitat to live

and reproduce. There are few other places in the world where you may come face to face with one of these large, harmless marine mammals. An estimated 300 to 700 manatees live in Belize, and to be effectively protected, they also need the indirect support of scuba divers.

Beyond this coastal area are the waters most prized by divers, those of the barrier reefs of Belize, which run parallel to the coast at a distance of 3 to 40 miles (5 to 60 kilometers) and create underwater formations with over a thousand cayes (little coral islands with a wealth of vegetation) scattered in the sea. Of the approximately one hundred species of stony corals in the Caribbean, as many as seventy-four of them can be found here, as well as thirty-six species of alcyonarians— primarily of the genuses *Alcyonaria* and *Gorgonia*—which are also known as soft corals, or octocorallia. Of the former, the most common are brain coral, star coral, staghorn coral (*Acropora cervicornis*), elkhorn coral (*Acropora palmata*), and the

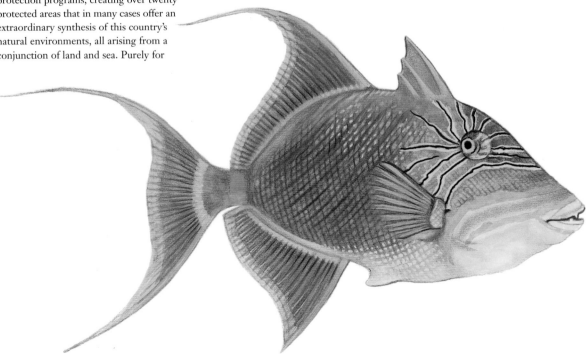

massive pillar corals (*Dendrogyra* sp.) that often dominate in Honduras, creating underwater scenes that resemble ancient temples with crumbling columns. Among them live other species typical of the underwater panoramas of the Caribbean: gorgonians with their great fans, sea plumes, deepwater red gorgonians, fire corals, black corals, and a variegated procession of multiform, multicolored sponges.

The reefs of Belize are not only rich in species but also offer, as does Australia's Great Barrier Reef, a wide variety of formations. Between Placencia and Punta Yacos, in the southern part of the country, are fringing reefs formed of a few species of corals that are more tolerant of fresh or murky water from nearby rivers. Near Victoria Channel, off Starn Creek, ring-shaped reefs (faro reef systems), rare in the Caribbean, create miniature atolls surrounding small lagoons.

There are even real atolls, a peculiarity of Belize, that create some of the most beautiful diving locations. Glover's Reef, Turneffe Islands, and Lighthouse Reef are unique environments, even without

considering the Caribbean's most famous Blue Hole. Located at Lighthouse, this is an ancient, immense grotto whose roof has collapsed, creating an abyss that plunges down to 415 feet (126 meters) deep, with a diameter of almost a quarter of a mile.

If you leave the numerous sandy floors, you will find every representative of the Caribbean fish population. French grunts (*Haemulon flavolineatum*), with their elegant blue-striped yellow bodies, swim in dense schools that suddenly make way for divers. There are large groupers, perhaps an *Epinephelus itajara*, or jewfish, which may reach up to 650 pounds (300 kg) in size. Farther on, ready to take the stage in a never-ending parade across the reef, are parrotfish, wrasses, butterflyfish, and angelfish. While less numerous and perhaps less colorful than their relatives in the Indopacific, their elegant movements never fail to attract the attention of scuba divers.

Some fish are notable for their strange forms, like the smooth trunkfish, the elongated scrawled filefish (*Aluterus scriptus*), the trumpetfish, the curious-looking pigfish with its strange dorsal fin

similar to a tuft of uncombed hair, the triggerfish, and numerous hamlets, distinguished scientifically by their coloration (striped, indigo, gray). Nurse sharks lie on the shadowy floor, while schools of glassfish or small groups of soldierfish and squirrelfish move slowly in the grottos, and large green morays make their dens in the cracks.

Every little corner hides surprises for anyone who knows where to look. Among the sponges lurk tiny blennies and little shrimp with long antennae, while luminescent gobies hover on the corals, garden eels poke out of the sand, and fairy basslets (*Gramma loreto*), with their two-tone yellow-and-fuchsia colors, swim among the gorgonians with bishop fish and seahorses.

The list of what the waters of Belize hold could go on and on, yet we would certainly forget some of the many life forms that scuba divers are likely to spot. As always, divers will be limited not so much by the inevitable laws of physics that govern the sport of scuba diving as by their ability to see and continue to marvel at the spectacle of nature.

Tiger shark
Galeocerdo cuvier

Recognizable by its short, wide nose and its caudal fin, whose upper lobe is bigger than its lower one. Blue-gray with dark vertical bars, which are more visible in young fish. Extremely dangerous; will come right into coastal, even brackish, waters. It is seen along the outer reef walls and off-shore barriers. Grows up to 18 feet (5.5 meters) in length.

ODONTASPIDIDAE FAMILY

Sand-tiger shark
Eugomphodus taurus

Robust, fusiform body and a flattened conical snout. The eyes are small and have no nictitating membrane. Large mouth, with long, sharp front teeth and molariform back teeth. Light brown, with dark spots scattered over the body. Lives in inshore waters near sandy seabeds, from the surface to a depth of 720 feet (220 meters). Feeds mainly on fish. Ovoviviparous; up to 10.4 feet (3.2 meters) in length.

GINGLYMOSTOMATIDAE FAMILY

Nurse shark
Ginglymostoma cirratum

Straight body flattened along the belly and close-set dorsal fins. Small mouth on the underside of its head, with a couple of short barbels. Yellowish gray in color; lives on the sandy seabed between the reefs, sheltered by big corals and caves. It grows up to 14 feet (4.3 meters) in length.

MYLIOBATIDAE FAMILY

Spotted eagle ray
◀ *Aetobatus narinari*

Ray with a lozenge-shaped body, big, pointed wings, and a pointed, convex head. The tail is almost three times as long as the body and has toothed spines along it. The back is dark in coloring with numerous light spots. The spotted eagle ray lives in the deep reef channels, close to shady beds. It grows up to 8.5 feet (2.5 meters) in width.

DASYATIDAE FAMILY

Southern stingray
▶ *Dasyatis americana*

Lozenge-shaped body, sometimes more pronounced than others; pointed nose and slightly pointed pectoral fins. A line of tubercules runs down the center of the back, and it has a long sharp spine in the front half of the tail. Tends to bury itself in the sand when resting on the seabed. Grayish black in color, the young being lighter than the adult specimens. It reaches a width of 5 feet (1.5 meters).

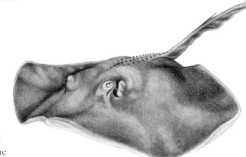

UROLOPHIDAE FAMILY

Yellow stingray
◀ *Urolophus jamaicensis*

Ray with a disc-shaped body, a rounded nose, and pectoral fin tips. The short tail has poisonous spines at the tip. Coloring is yellow-brown with dark markings of varying size. Lives on the sandy beds close to the reefs, where it buries itself. Up to 2.5 feet (76 centimeters) in width.

MURAENIDAE FAMILY

Purplemouth moray
Gymnothorax vicinus

This moray is recognizable by its yellowish eyes, its black-edged dorsal fin, and a mouth that is purple inside. Nocturnal, it lives on rocky seabeds and along reefs, including shallow ones. It grows up to 4 feet (1.2 meters).

▶

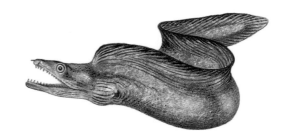

Green moray
Gymnothorax funebris

◀

Easily recognized by its greenish color, which varies in intensity from specimen to specimen but is always uniform. The green moray is a nocturnal animal, but during the day it hides in the reef crevices, often in shallow water, and can be easily approached. It may attack if excessively provoked. It grows up to 7.5 feet (2.3 meters) in length.

Spotted moray
Gymnothorax moringa

▶

This moray is common in shallow seabeds, often rich in vegetation, where it hides in crevices during the day, coming out at night to hunt. It is yellowish white with numerous brown or reddish black markings. It can grow up to 4 feet (1.2 meters) in length.

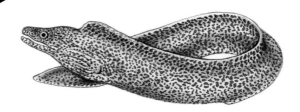

AULOSTOMIDAE FAMILY

Trumpetfish
Aulostomus maculatus

◀

Fish with an elongated body, tubular nose, and terminal mouth. There is a thin barbel underneath its lower jaw. The dorsal fin consists of a series of separate spiny rays. It lives close to reefs, where it camouflages itself by changing color and swimming in an almost vertical position. It is a timid fish and one which is hard to approach. It measures up to 3.3 feet (1 meter) in length.

FISTULARIIDAE FAMILY

Blue-spotted cornetfish
Fistularia tabacaria

▶

Elongated fish with tubular nose and terminal mouth. The two central rays of the tail fin are exceptionally elongated. Found near underwater meadows and reefs with sandy beds. Lives alone or in small groups. It grows up to 6 feet (1.8 meters).

SYNODONTIDAE FAMILY

Sand diver
Synodus intermedius ▶

Robust, elongated body, flattened underbelly. Wide mouth showing its small but numerous teeth. Has a dark blotch on the operculum and yellowish lengthwise stripes along its sides. Lives on sandy seabeds in which it buries itself. Grows up to 1.8 feet (55 centimeters) long.

MEGALOPIDAE FAMILY

◀ ### Tarpon
Megalops atlanticus

Big, robust-bodied fish. Oblique, upward-angled mouth. Silvery body covered in large scales. The last ray of the dorsal fin is long and threadlike. Lives in surface waters where there is very little light. Measures up to 8.5 feet (2.5 meters) long.

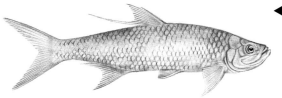

ALBULIDAE FAMILY

Bonefish
Albula vulpes ▶

Tapered body with pointed nose and well-developed, downward-angling mouth. The last ray on the dorsal and anal fins is filament-shaped. Tends to come into the coastal sandy beds with the tide. Found on coral seabeds with abundant sandy areas and reef channels. Grows up to 3.3 feet (1 meter).

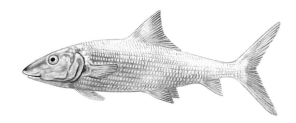

SPHYRAENIDAE FAMILY

◀ ### Great barracuda
Sphyraena barracuda

Tapering, sub-cylindrical body with a long, pointed snout and prominent lower jaw. The two dorsal fins are clearly separate. The caudal fin is slightly lunar-shaped, with pointed lobes. Coloring is silvery with dark vertical bands and small spots near the caudal fin. Lives in coastal waters above coral, sandy or meadowland seabeds. Measures up to 6.5 feet (2 meters).

SCORPAENIDAE FAMILY

Spotted scorpionfish
Scorpaena plumieri ▶

Powerfully-bodied scorpionfish with growths and appendices on its nose. It is greeny-brown with reddish shading. There are three dark vertical bars on the tail. The inside of the pectoral fins is dark with small white marks. This is one of the most common scorpionfish found on coral reefs, growing up to 16 inches (40 centimeters).

ANTENNARIIDAE FAMILY

Ocellated frogfish
Antennarius ocellatus ▶

Very similar to the previous fish, distinguished from it by three ocellar marks: one lateral, one dorsal, and one caudal. Lives in rocky, coralline habitats, as well as on sandy and muddy bottoms. Color varies from brownish red to brownish yellow. Measures up to 15 inches (38 centimeters).

SYNGNATHIDAE FAMILY

◀ ### Lined seahorse
Hippocampus erectus

This fish's uniquely shaped body is made up of bony rings, on which its head is set at an angle. It is found in areas rich in vegetation where it camouflages itself by anchoring itself to the algae with its prehensile tail. It grows up to 7 inches (17 centimeters).

HOLOCENTRIDAE FAMILY

Longspine squirrelfish
Holocentrus rufus ▶

Compressed, oval body; the front part of the dorsal fin has robust, white-tipped, spiny rays, and the back part is exceptionally deep. During the daytime it hides in the reef crevices, coming out at night to hunt for mollusks, crustaceans, and echinoderms. Measures up to 11.5 inches (28 centimeters).

◀ ### Blackbar soldierfish
Myripristis jacobus

Oval-bodied fish with a big head and large eyes. Red body with a black bar covering the rear edge of the opercula. Stays hidden in caves in the daytime, where it swims upside down because of the light reflecting off the seabed. It measures up to 8 inches (20 centimeters).

Squirrelfish
Holocentrus ascensionis ▶

Very similar to the previous fish, distinguished mainly by its yellowish-green dorsal fin. Stays in the darker areas of the reef in the daytime. Likes shallow coral seabeds with abundant crevices and small caves. Measures up to 14 inches (35 centimeters).

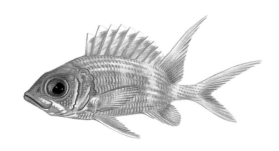

Glasseye snapper
Heteropriacanthus cruentatus

Robust, compressed body with a square head and oblique mouth angled upward. Very large eyes. Reddish with silvery vertical bars that disappear on the back. Prefers surface waters, where it tends to inhabit the less illuminated areas during the day. Measures up to 12 inches (30 centimeters).

CIRRHITIDAE FAMILY

Redspotted hawkfish
Amblycirrhitus pinos

▶

Small fish with a deep body and pointed nose. The spiny rays of the dorsal fin have fringed points. It has distinctive red spots on the nose, the back, and the dorsal fin. Lives on reefs where it waits in ambush, resting on the seabed. Measures up to 4.4 inches (11 centimeters).

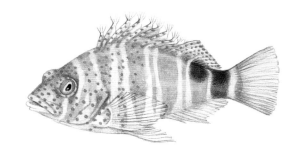

SERRANIDAE FAMILY

Jewfish
Epinephelus itajara

◀ One of the biggest of the Atlantic groupers, with a wide, flat head. It is greenish gray in color with small black marks. It usually makes its den in caves or wrecks, and its sheer size—it grows up to 8 feet (2.4 meters)—makes it a potentially dangerous fish.

Red grouper
Epinephelus morio

▶

Sturdy fish with a tapered body. The second spiny ray on the dorsal fin is bigger than the others. Concave caudal fin with pointed lobes in adult fish. Often stays immobile on the seabed to camouflage itself. Measures up to 3 feet (90 centimeters).

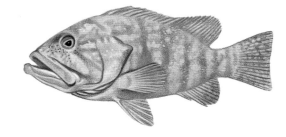

Nassau grouper
Epinephelus striatus

◀ Grouper with tapered body and small pelvic fins. Common on coral seabeds, where it rarely strays from the area immediately around its den. It changes color rapidly if frightened or its interest is aroused. Shoals of thousands form in small areas for spawning. It grows up to 3.3 feet (1 meter) in length. Wide-spread from North Carolina to Brazil.

Coney
Cephalopholis fulva ▶

Tapered body. The caudal fin, whether straight-edged or slightly rounded, always has distinct corners. Coloring tends to differ with depth. A gregarious species that prefers reefs and abounds in crevices. Will allow divers to approach slowly. Grows up to 16 inches (40 centimeters).

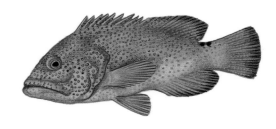

Greater soapfish
◀ **Greater soapfish**
Rypticus saponaceus

This fish has a pointed front profile, flattened on the back of the head. The dorsal fin is set back and has a rounded rear edge. Lives in shallow water close to reefs and on sandy beds. If startled it secretes a mucus that is poisonous to other fish. Measures up to 13 inches (33 centimeters).

Butter hamlet
Butter hamlet ▶
Hypoplectrus unicolor

Deep, compressed, body. Lower edge of the pre-operculum is finely toothed. Has a distinct saddle-shaped mark on the caudal peduncle. Prefers coral reefs, where it swims close to the seabed. Measures up to 5 inches (13 centimeters).

Indigo hamlet
◀ **Indigo hamlet**
Hypoplectrus indigo

Similar to the previous species, from which it is distinguished by its bluish color and vertical white bars. Prefers coral seabeds, where it swims close to the bottom. Like the other species, this one can also be approached slowly. Measures up to 5 inches (13 centimeters).

Tobaccofish
Tobaccofish ▶
Serranus tabacarius

Tapering body with a broad, horizontal, brown-orange stripe. Lives close to the seabed on the border between reefs and sandy seabeds or ones strewn with reef detritus. Tends to become gregarious at depths greater than 165 feet (50 meters). Measures up to 7.5 inches (18 centimeters).

Peppermint bass
Liopropoma rubre

Small fish with tapering body and double dorsal fin. The tip of the dorsal, anal, and tail fins are the same color. The flanks have red stripes. Tends to stay hidden in crevices and hollows and is for this reason not often seen, although it is common. Measures up to 3.2 inches (8 centimeters).

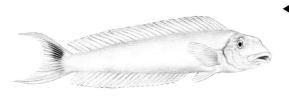

GRAMMATIDAE FAMILY

Fairy basslet
Gramma loreto

Small fish with highly characteristic coloring, half purple and half yellow. Lives in small schools in hollows and crevices where it swims upside down because of the reflected light. Measures up to 3.2 inches (8 centimeters).

APOGONIDAE FAMILY

Flamefish
Apogon maculatus

Small fish with a robust, oval body and a deep caudal peduncle. Bright red with a black spot on the operculum and at the base of the second dorsal fin. Prefers surface waters, where it stays inside caves during the day. Measures up to 5 inches (13 centimeters).

MALACANTHIDAE FAMILY

Sand tilefish
Malacanthus plumieri

Elongated body with very large lips. Crescent-shaped tail with pointed lobes. Yellowish blue with yellow and blue stripes on the head. Tail is often yellow. Lives on sandy and rubble-strewn seabeds, where it digs itself a den. Measures up to 2 feet (60 centimeters).

CENTROPOMIDAE FAMILY

Snook
Centropomus undecimalis

Robust body terminating in a pointed head, the dorsal fin has a very angled profile. The lateral line is dark and continues right to the rear edge of the tail. Lives in coastal waters where there are plenty of mangroves. Measures up to 4.3 feet (1.3 meters).

Crevalle jack
Caranx hippos

Has a deep, elongated body, very tapered and convex at the front. Thin, characteristically forked tail. The young fish are gregarious and more common in coastal waters, while adult specimens tend to be solitary. Commoner in open water and along the outer edge of the reef. Measures up to 3.5 feet (1 meter).

Bar jack
Carangoides ruber

Elongated, tapering, silvery body, marked by a dark band at the base of the dorsal fin that stretches to the lower caudal lobe. Lives in shoals of variable size and often follows schools of mullet and stingray to feed on invertebrates they uncover. Measures up to 2 feet (60 centimeters).

Rainbow runner
Elagatis bipinnulata

Elongated, spindle-shaped body with two light blue, horizontal stripes separated by a green or yellowish streak. Common in open water, this fish often moves close to the outer slopes of the reef. Lives in shoals and seems to be attracted by the air bubbles produced by scuba-diving equipment. Measures up to 4 feet (1.2 meters).

Palometa
Trachinotus goodei

Carangid with lozenge-shaped body, distinguished by large rays on the dorsal and anal fins. Silver with three to five vertical black streaks. Lives in coastal waters among coral formations. Measures up to 20 inches (50 centimeters).

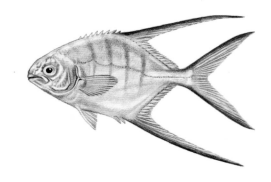

LUTJANIADAE FAMILY

Yellowtail snapper
Ocyurus chrysurus

▶

Elongated body with pronounced forked tail and pointed lobes. Purplish blue color with a horizontal yellow stripe and small spots. Swims alone or in small groups close to the reef or to meadowlands. More active at night. Measures up to 2.5 feet (75 centimeters).

◀ Mutton snapper
Lutjanus analis

Robust, deep body, olive colored with blackish streaks that are more marked in fish up to 16 inches (40 centimeters). The adult fish prefer rocky and coral seabeds, while the younger ones are more often found on sandy beds and in seaweed meadows. Measures up to 2.5 feet (75 centimeters).

Cubera snapper
Lutjanus cyanopterus

▶

Tapered but robust body, grayish with reddish reflections at the front. Large lips. Prefers rather deep rocky and coral seabeds. Young fish are more common along the shoreline. Measures up to 5.5 feet (1.6 meters).

HAEMULIDAE FAMILY

Porkfish
Anisotremus virginicus

◀

Compressed body, very deep at the front. The fish has two dark vertical bars on the head and a series of blue and yellow horizontal streaks. Swims alone or in small groups, which are more common above the reef during the day. The young act as cleaner fish. Measures up to 16 inches (40 centimeters).

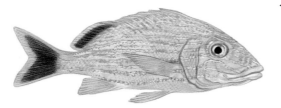

Bluestriped grunt
Haemulon sciurus

Deep, compressed body, the rear part of which is dark colored, including the dorsal and tail fins. Background color is yellowish with numerous horizontal blue stripes. Forms large schools near the coast on rocky or sandy seabeds. Measures up to 18 inches (45 centimeters).

French grunt
Haemulon flavolineatum

Deep body with pointed snout and small mouth. Yellowish with numerous blue streaks, horizontal above the lateral line and oblique below. Prefers coral seabeds, where it forms schools of up to a thousand fish. Likes poorly illuminated areas. Measures up to 12 inches (30 centimeters).

SCIAENIDAE FAMILY

Reef croaker
Odontoscion dentex

Elongated, compressed body with a big, oblique terminal mouth. Reddish body with a black blotch at the base of the pelvic fin. Prefers rocky habitats and shallow coral reefs, tending to stay in poorly lit areas. Measures up to 10 inches (25 centimeters).

Jackknife fish
Equetus lanceolatus

Deep front body section and very pointed rear section. Characteristically deep forward dorsal fin, especially in the young. Dark bar runs from the tip of the dorsal fin to the tail. Prefers the darker parts of reefs and hollows. Measures up to 10 inches (25 centimeters).

High-hat
Pareques acuminatus ▶

Deep-bodied at the front end, then stumpy with a well-defined dorsal fin and not so deep rear part. Reddish brown with longitudinal whitish stripes. Prefers surface waters close to rocky and coral bottoms, near caves and poorly illuminated areas. Measures up to 9 inches (23 centimeters).

KYPHOSIDAE FAMILY

◀ ### Bermuda chub
Kyphosus sectatrix

Deep, oval body with a small terminal mouth. Grayish in color with thin bronze horizontal stripes. Tends to form schools close to coral and rocky seabeds rich in algae. Measures up to 2.5 feet (76 centimeters).

MULLIDAE FAMILY

Yellow goatfish
Mulloidichthys martinicus

Tapered body; the snout has a slightly convex and pointed edge. Olive-colored back with light-colored flanks, bearing a horizontal yellow bar stretching right to the tail. Forms small schools on the sandy beds close to reefs. Measures up to 16 inches (40 centimeters).

◀ ### Spotted goatfish
Pseudopeneus maculatus

Tapered body with a slightly pointed snout. The edge of the operculum has a spine that is quite pronunced in some cases. There are three large blackish blotches on the sides of the body. Forms small groups of four to six fish to hunt. Grows up to 10.5 inches (26 centimeters).

EPHIPPIDAE FAMILY

Atlantic spadefish
Chaetodipterus faber ▶

Very deep, compressed body; the lobes of the dorsal and anal fins are very elongated rearward. Grayish with four to five dark, vertical, bands. Forms small schools that swim in open waters some way from the reef. Sometimes spontaneously approaches divers. Grows up to 3 feet (90 centimeters).

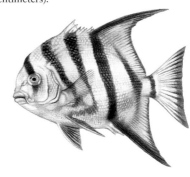

Foureye butterflyfish
Chaetodon capistratus ▶

Butterflyfish with deep, compressed body with yellow fins and a small black spot on the rear edge of the dorsal fin. Tends to become dark at night. Usually swims in pairs close to reefs and rocky seabeds. Grows up to 8 inches (20 centimeters) .

◀ ### Reef butterflyfish
Chaetodon sedentarius

Deep, compressed body, almost vertical rear profile. Yellowish coloring, with a dark, wide band at the rear of its body, running from the dorsal to the anal fin. Prefers coral bottoms, where it goes as deep as 300 feet (90 meters). Measures up to 6 inches (15 centimeters).

Spotfin butterflyfish
Chaetodon ocellatus ▶

Deep, compressed body, with yellow fins and a small black mark on the rear edge of the dorsal fin. Tends to turn a darker color at night. Generally swims in pairs close to reefs and rocky bottoms. Maximum size 8 inches (20 centimeters).

◀ ### Longsnout butterflyfish
Chaetodon aculeatus

Compressed, very deep body thanks to the dorsal fin, which has well-developed spiny rays. Long, pointed snout. Solitary, preferring the deepest coral seabeds and reef crevices where it takes shelter if frightened. Measures up to 4 inches (10 centimeters).

Banded butterflysifh
Chaetodon striatus ▶

Deep, compressed body, whitish in color with three dark slanting bars, the first of which hides the eye. Young fish have an ocellar marking on the caudal peduncle. Lives alone or in pairs, close to the coral. Measures up to 6.5 inches (16 centimeters).

POMACANTHIDAE FAMILY

Gray angelfish ▶
Pomacanthus arcuatus

Angelfish with deep, compressed body; the dorsal and caudal lobes are pointed at the rear. The tail fin has a straight trailing edge. Grayish brown in color, with a very pale mouth. Lives alone or in pairs in the richest areas of the reef. Measures up to 20 inches (50 centimeters).

French angelfish ◀
Pomacanthus paru

Angelfish with rounded, compressed body; rear lobes of the dorsal and anal fins are very pointed. Blackish in color with yellow markings on the snout and the pectoral fins. Prefers the parts of the reef closest to the surface, rich in gorgonians. Measures up to 12 inches (30 centimeters).

Rock beauty ▶
Holacanthus tricolor

A territorial species, it never abandons its territory, defending it against all attacks. If approached, it will swim away, then return slowly. It measures up to 8 inches (20 centimeters).

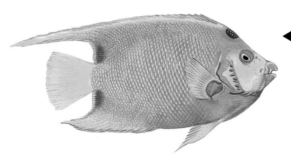

Queen angelfish ◀
Holacanthus ciliaris

Angelfish with deep, compressed body; the rear lobes of the dorsal and anal fins are very pointed and extend backward past the trailing edge of the caudal fin. Yellow, densely spotted with blue on the sides, with a blotch of the same color on the head. Lives on the parts of the reef closest to the surface and the deepest parts, over 165 feet (50 meters). Measures up to 18 inches (45 centimeters).

Cherubfish ▶
Centropyge argi

Small, oval-bodied angelfish with yellow markings on the head and part of the back, and blue sides, belly, and tail. Prefers the deepest parts of the coral bed, usually over 100 feet (30 meters), where it sometimes forms small groups. Measures up to 3.2 inches (8 centimeters).

Blue chromis
Chromis cyanea

Small, oval-bodied fish with deeply cleft tail fin. Bluish with black-edged caudal lobes. Quite common around the reef, where it forms schools. Measures up to 5 inches (13 centimeters).

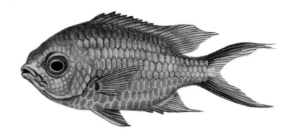

Beaugregory
Stegastes leucostictus

Small fish, slightly oval in shape; forked tail with rounded lobes. Brownish in color with a lighter or yellowish tail. Territorial species, prefers sandy seabeds or ones rich in algae and detritus. Measures up to 4 inches (10 centimeters).

Yellowtail damselfish
Microspathodon chrysurus

Small fish with a robust, brownish body, with small blue markings and a distinctive yellow tail. The young fish tend to stay among the branches of fire corals, sometimes as cleaner fish. Adults occupy small territories in the parts of the reef closest to the surface. Measures up to 8.4 inches (21 centimeters).

Brown chromis
Chromis multilineata

Grey, swarthy-colored fish with a black spot at the base of the pectoral fins and yellow tips to the dorsal fin and the caudal lobes. Lives in groups above coral formations. Measures up to 7 inches (17 centimeters).

Bicolor damselfish
Stegastes partitus

Small fish with a compressed, oval-shaped body and a small terminal mouth. Dark-colored front section of the body and white at the back. Lives close to the higher parts of the reef, where it establishes its territory, which it defends from other fishes of the same species. Measures up to 5 inches (12 centimeters).

Three-spot damselfish ▶
Stegastes planifrons

Small fish with compressed, oval body and small terminal mouth. Dark in color with yellow-rimmed eyes and black spots at the base of the pectoral fins and the caudal peduncle. Lives close to the parts of the reef nearest to the surface—which are richer in algae—where it establishes its own territory and defends it tenaciously from all comers, including divers. Measures up to 5 inches (12 centimeters).

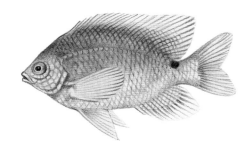

◀ ### Sergeant major
Abudefduf saxatilis

Compressed, ovoid, deep body covered with rough scales, which extend to the fins. Silvery white with dark vertical bars and a yellow stripe at the base of the dorsal fin. Lives in schools in the parts of the reef closest to the surface. Measures up to 8 inches (20 centimeters).

LABRIDAE FAMILY

Spotfin hogfish ▶
Bodianus pulchellus

Robust body and pointed snout. The dorsal and anal fins have pointed rear lobes. The adult fish are almost totally red except for the tail and part of the caudal fin, which are yellow. Generally more common on coral reefs at 65 feet (20 meters) or deeper. Measures up to 8 inches (20 centimeters).

◀ ### Hogfish
Lachnolaimus maximus

Fairly large member of the Labridae family with a pointed head. Recognizable principally by the first rays of the dorsal fin, which are very developed. Whitish, with a dark bar along the back, stretching from the mouth to the tail. Prefers sandy seabeds, where it likes to dig for its prey. Measures up to 3 feet (90 centimeters).

Bluehead wrasse ▶
Thalassoma bifasciatum

Elongated, compressed body, with coloring that varies greatly according to age. In adults the body is greenish at the rear and bluish at the front with black and white stripes in between. The young fish are yellowish. It is found in a great number of different habitats. Measures up to 7 inches (18 centimeters).

Puddingwife
Halichoeres radiatus

Very deep body, blue-green in color, with yellow-edged caudal fin. This is an uncommon fish and is hard to approach, as it swims continuously and is also very suspicious. Measures up to 20 inches (50 centimeters).

SCARIDAE FAMILY

Blue parrotfish
Scarus coeruleus

Tapered, robust body. Adult males have a frontal bump that modifies the front profile of the snout. Mainly blue in color. Feeds principally on algae, and for this reason it moves swiftly from one part of the reef to another. Measures up to 3 feet (90 centimeters).

Queen parrotfish
Scarus vetula

Blue-green parrotfish with scales edged in pinkish orange. The nose has broad blue stripes around the mouth and close to the eyes. Lives on coral reefs up to 85 feet (25 meters) in depth and measures up to 2 feet (60 centimeters).

Stoplight parrotfish
Sparisoma viride

Mainly green in color, with yellowish orange slanting bars on its head and on the caudal fin and a yellow mark on the operculum. Reasonably common where coral seabeds alternate with areas rich in algae. Measures up to 20 inches (50 centimeters).

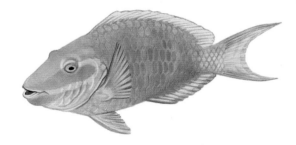

OPISTOGNATHIDAE FAMILY

Yellowhead jawfish
Opistognathus aurifrons

Small, bottom-dwelling fish with elongated, tapering body ending in a short but powerful head, with large eyes. Coloring is blue with a yellowish head. Lives on the bottom of the ocean close to a den it digs for itself, ready to take shelter. Measures up to 4 inches (10 centimeters).

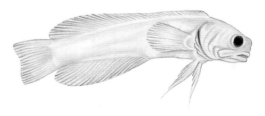

BLENNIIDAE FAMILY

Red-mouthed blenny
Ophioblennius atlanticus ▶

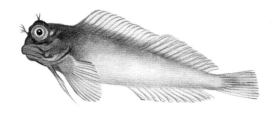

Blenny with compressed body and blunt nose. The mouth has distinctive big lips. Dark in color, with yellow or pink shading on the pectoral and caudal fins. A territorial fish, it prefers rocky seabeds and the parts of the reef closest to the surface. Measures up to 5 inches (13 centimeters).

GOBIIDAE FAMILY

◀ ### Neon goby
Gobiosoma oceanops

Small goby, easily recognizable by its dark coloring, on which two fluorescent blue horizontal stripes stand out. Cleaner fish, which forms groups with others of its species in characteristic cleaning stations. Measures up to 2 inches (5 centimeters).

PEMPHERIDAE FAMILY

Glassy sweeper
Pempheris schomburgki ▶

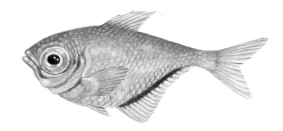

Small fish with compressed, oval body, tapered at the rear. Silvery pink color, with a very long black-edged anal fin. Lives in schools inside grottoes or in reef crevices, from which it emerges at night. Measures up to 6.5 inches (16 centimeters).

ACANTHURIDAE FAMILY

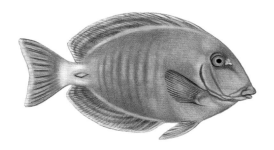

◀ ### Doctorfish
Acanthurus chirurgus

Surgeonfish with deep, compressed body with a distinctive set of dark vertical bars, sometimes more clearly visible than others. This species usually lives alone, or with other surgeonfish, close to the reef. Measures up to 10 inches (25 centimeters).

Blue tang
Acanthurus coeruleus ▶

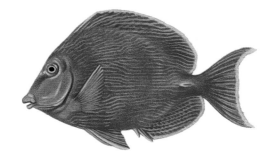

Surgeonfish that is bluish in color, with lighter fins. The cutting laminae typical of surgeonfish can be seen on the caudal peduncle. If frightened, it can change color rapidly. It tends to be solitary, but may gather in dense schools, mingling with other surgeonfish. Up to 10 inches (25 centimeters) in length.

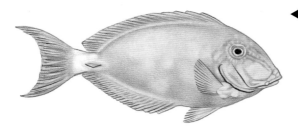

Ocean surgeonfish
Acanthurus bahianus

Surgeonfish with coloring varying from bluish gray to dark brown. Light-colored spokes surround the eyes. Prefers flat or slightly sloping coral seabeds. Measures up to 14 inches (35 centimeters).

BOTHIDAE FAMILY

Peacock flounder
Bothus lunatus

Identifiable by the series of ocellar spots on the body and the small bluish marks on the fins. Has a very elongated pelvic fin that is often kept erect. Lives on sandy seabeds or ones covered in detritus, where its ability to change color enables it to camouflage itself. Measures up to 16 inches (40 centimeters).

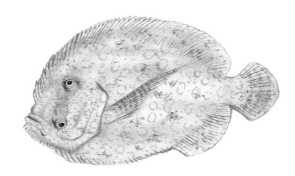

BALISTIDAE FAMILY

Gray triggerfish
Balistes capriscus

Grayish triggerfish, with small bluish spots on the back and fins. Lives alone or in small groups near rocky seabeds or areas rich in vegetation. Measures up to 12 inches (30 centimeters).

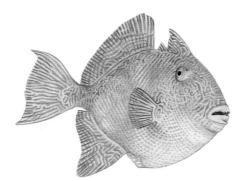

Queen triggerfish
Balistes vetula

Triggerfish that has dorsal and caudal fins with elongated and pointed lobes. It is characterized by a pair of blue stripes on the snout and blue stripes on the odd-numbered fins. Lives on coralline seabeds broken by wide sandy and detrital areas, at depths of from 6.5 feet (2 meters) to over 165 feet (50 meters). Up to 2 feet (60 centimeters) in length.

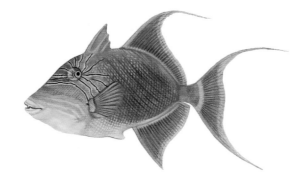

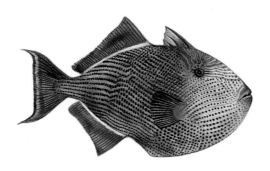

Black durgon
Melichthys niger

Bluish black body with bluish stripes at the base of the dorsal and anal fins. Lives in small groups along the outer reef wall, to depths of 200 feet (60 meters). Measures up to 20 inches (50 centimeters).

MONACANTHIDAE FAMILY

Scrawled filefish
Aluteres scriptus

Tapered body with pointed snout and broad tail. Coloring characterized by irregular streaks and small blue markings. A solitary fish, it lives in both lagoons and along the outer reef wall, from where it heads for the open sea. Measures up to 3.5 feet (1.1 meters).

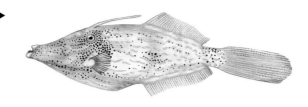

OSTRACIIDAE FAMILY

Smooth trunkfish
Lactophrys triqueter

Fish with a triangular-shaped silhouette. Has large hexagonal bony scales. Is dark with numerous lighter-colored marks. Usually a solitary fish, it does sometimes form small groups. Prefers coral seabeds, although it can be found on sandy ones. Measures up to 12 inches (30 centimeters).

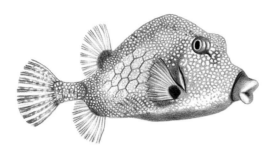

TETRAODONTIDAE FAMILY

Bandtail pufferfish
Sphoeroides spengleri

Elongated body, rounded at the front. The large nostrils are easily spotted on the head. A horizontal series of marks runs along the sides below the lateral line. This fish nearly always swims close to the seabed, whether meadowlands, coral, or detritus-strewn. Measures up to 7 inches (18 centimeters).

Checkered pufferfish
Sphoeroides testudineus

Round, spindle-shaped body, marked with light-colored geometrical lines making a kind of grid. Prefers coastal bays, rocks, and meadowlands. Not often found close to reefs. Measures up to 12 inches (30 centimeters).

Longnose pufferfish
Canthigaster rostrata

Small pufferfish with a very pointed nose and a small terminal mouth. Dark coloring on the back, yellowish along the sides. Blue streaks and marks around the eyes, close to the mouth, and on the tail. Prefers coral seabeds and meadowlands. Measures up to 4.5 inches (11 centimeters).

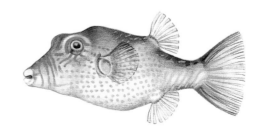

Invertebrates

Sea fan
Gorgonia ventalina

Gorgonian forming large fans of considerable size, connected to each other by more compact and thinner branches. Usually purple in color, it measures up to 6.5 feet (2 meters).

Elkhorn coral
Acropora palmata

These colonies have very apparent but flattened ramifications. The surface is dotted with small tubular corallites and will break easily if knocked. It measures up to 12 feet (3.6 meters).

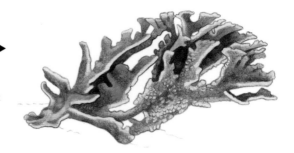

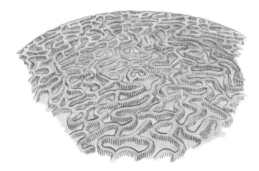

Brain coral
Colpophyllia natans

Forms large, rounded masses, the surface decorated with circumvolute raised formations. The polyps open at night. It measures up to 7 feet (2.1 meters).

Azure vase sponge
Callyspongia plicifera

A sponge shaped like a hollow vase with the external surface made up of numerous raised circumvolutional folds with a fluorescent coloring, it grows alone or in small groups. It measures up to 20 inches (50 centimeters).

Touch-me-not sponge
Neofibularia nolimetangere

A brown-colored sponge, massive and of varying shape. The external surface is similar to thick felt. If touched, it will cause a sharp stinging rash. Treat with vinegar. It measures up to 3.5 feet (1 meter).

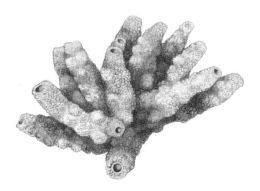

Branching tube sponge
Pseudoceratina crassa

This sponge is made up of numerous tubes dotted with small protuberances. The tubes originate from a common base and have a large pore at the tip. It measures up to 16 inches (40 centimeters).

Stove-pipe sponge
Aplysina archeri

This sponge is composed of long hollow tubes originating from a common base. The walls are thin and soft to the touch. It appears as isolated colonies, measures up to 5.5 feet (1.7 meters).

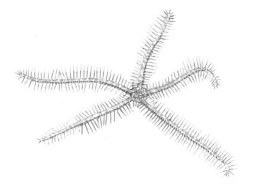

Brittle star
Ophiothrix sp.

Has long flexible arms marked by numerous side spikes and lives mainly on sponges. It measures up to 4 inches (10 centimeters).

Cushion sea star
Oreaster reticulatus

This large starfish has a massive regular form. The upper part is decorated with rounded needles forming a geometric pattern. It lives on sandy seabeds, and measures up to 16 inches (40 centimeters).

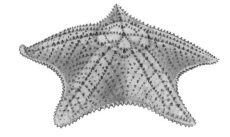

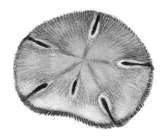

Sand dollar
Mellita sexieperforata

This sea urchin has a disc shape, the body perforated by six apertures. It lives on the sand close to the reef, emerging at night. It measures up to 4 inches (10 centimeters).

Cover

*On the sea floor
off Roatan,*

*Top left
A sergeant major fish
(Abudefduf saxatilis).*

Back cover

*Top
A dolphin lets a few
scuba divers
approach him in the
waters off Anthony's
Key Resort.*

*Center
A small grouper.*

*Bottom
The drawing
reconstructs the dive
at Sayonara, on the
atoll of Turneffe.*

Credit photographer

*All photographs by Roberto Rinaldi
Dive Drawings: Domitilla Müller/Archivio White Star
Marine Life Charts: Monica Falcone/Archivio White Star*

Technical Editor: Stacey Kronquest of Rodale's Scuba Diving
Production Editor: Kerrie Baldwin
Text Designer: Barbara Balch

SPECIAL THANKS:
Many people helped us in the realization of this book. A token of sincere thanks goes to Helena Norman for her great help in providing us with the necessary documentation. We are also thankful to Vanna Cammelli, owner of Aquadiving Tours, who worked hard and planned our travels toward the most different destinations. In Belize, we owe much to Annie Crawley, a very good photographer and skilled guide who showed us the best places and the most hidden creatures. We express our gratitude to the crew of the *Wave Dancer*, the beautiful Peter Hughes' boat: Thanks to Captain Paul Keating, to Andrea Bill, Eugene Leslie, Charles P. Noralez, and Ryan Vernon, who has taken care of logistics. The Lighthouse Reef Resort staff has welcomed us graciously and has proven to have a deep knowledge of their beautiful sea beds. A particular thank-you to the manager, Bret Wolfenbarger. Guiseppe D'Amato's, Luciano Stefani's, and Paolo Vitale's diving center TGI has welcomed us to the Bay Islands. A particular thank-you to Alessandro Boccuccia, expert guide to the sea beds of the islands. Thanks to the staff of the Agressor Fleet, a great help to us in searching for peculiar documentation.